Fortysomething and Single

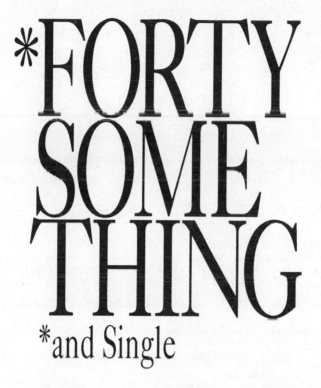

*FORTY SOME THING
*and Single

HAROLD IVAN SMITH

VICTOR BOOKS®
A DIVISION OF SCRIPTURE PRESS PUBLICATIONS INC.
USA CANADA ENGLAND

Library of Congress Cataloging-in-Publication Data

Smith, Harold Ivan, 1947–
    Fortysomething and single / by Harold Ivan Smith.
    p.   cm.
    ISBN 0-89693-185-4
    1. Single people — United States. 2. Middle aged persons — United States. 3. Single people — United States — Religious life. 4. Middle aged persons — United States — Religious life.   I. Title.
HQ800.4.U6S635 1991
305.9'0652 — dc20   90-22849
                                                          CIP

Contents

1. Fortysomething and Still Single   7

2. Every Day . . . In Every Way   I'm Getting Older   19

3. There's More to Being Forty and Single
   Than Waiting for the Right One to Show Up   35

4. Keep in the Middle of the Road   47

5. Shaping a Fortysomething Faith   60

6. Life Is Hard But God Is Good   73

7. Marching Off the Map   87

8. Beyond This Point . . . There Be Dragons!   100

9. There's More to Having It All
   Than Having It All   111

10. Heroes in an Age of Celebrities   124

11. Where Will You Be When You Get
    to Where You're Going?   137

Appendix A   Friend of a Fortysomething Survey   **151**

Appendix B   Fortysomething Book List   **154**

Appendix C   Forty Literary Friends for Fortysomethings **157**

Notes   **160**

Chapter One

FORTYSOMETHING AND STILL SINGLE

I am forty now, and forty years is a lifetime;
it is extremely old age. To go on living
after forty is unseemly, disgusting, immoral!
Who goes on living after forty? Give me a
sincere and honest answer! I'll tell you —
fools and rogues.
— *Dostoyevsky*

**GOAL FOR FORTYSOMETHINGS: To admit that I
am a fortysomething.**

I remember the moment all the commotion about turning
forty began. While speaking to a group of yuppies at a conference in Washington, D.C., I hit upon a new illustration to
emphasize the point I was making. Ah, I thought to myself, a
perfect example for this group of D.C.'s finest.

"It is somewhat like what you felt when you heard that
John Kennedy had been assassinated," I explained.

I was taken back by the laughter. I know the gleam of
Camelot has been tarnished considerably by recent revelations
about Kennedy's personal life, but I had not expected
laughter.

"There's nothing funny about John Kennedy being assassinated!" I said sternly.

"Dr. Smith," a man in the front row interrupted, "most of

us were less than two years old when that happened. We can't remember how we felt." My face caved in.

With the laughter that swept the room it seemed, for a few moments, that I was in an echo chamber. I felt as if I was a victim of one of those Hollywood special effects: out of my body I hovered about three feet over the room, observing the scene. The laughter built to a crescendo with my stunned surprise.

"Take me to the hotel; it's past my bedtime," I joked.

It took a long time to go to sleep that night. I had *aged.* Instantly. Until that moment at the conference, I had regarded myself as a young man.

No more. Now I realized there was a new generation in place. And I was not part of it. Without warning, I was "old." Just like that. As the Bible says, "in the twinkling of an eye."

A few weeks later over dinner I was discussing the summer's hit movie, *Dragnet,* patterned after the popular TV series of the fifties. As a boy, "Dragnet" had been one of my favorites. The cool and aloof Sargeant Friday was my hero.

"Yeah," my dinner companion replied, "My dad used to watch 'Dragnet' before I was born."

"Before I was born?" This was not a teen or a college student, but a young adult, a professional. And his father watched "Dragnet" *before* he was born! Pass the Geritol.

These two incidents had a particular impact on me because only a few weeks earlier I had laughed at a friend's faux pas. As he approached his seventieth birthday he had been invited to speak to a large audience and was "holding court" as only he could.

"Why the other day," he started into a story, "I was in Paris. . . . " And he noticed his wife's vigorous frown.

Well, it had not been the other day, literally, but in the sense that speakers use that phrase. My friend stopped then started again, "Well, a few years ago . . . "

Again his wife shook her head.

As if only he and his wife were present, he confessed sadly, "I haven't been in Paris in twenty-five years . . . " The laughter of the audience brought him back to reality.

"Ah, let's say, the last time I was in Paris . . . "

Some friends and I had laughed over that episode. Now I understood for the first time the zing of that old adage, "Time flies."

TIME FLIES

I remember my thirty-ninth birthday better than my fortieth. A couple of colleagues invited me to dinner and ordered a marvelous cake that came complete with singing waiters. While they were making a ruckus, I was looking for the nearest exit.

"He's thirty-nine!" One waiter called out to the crowded restaurant.

"Whoooo!" swept across the restaurant.

"The big one cometh," someone shouted.

"Better enjoy it while you can!"

There were a few veiled references to something about "being over the hill," a phrase that I would hear more frequently in the course of the next twelve months.

As I sliced the cake, one of my friends, looked up and said, "You know, don't you, that this really is your fortieth?"

"What are you saying?" I asked.

"Well, a birthday comes at the end of a year. Your first birthday came at the *end* of your first year."

"So?"

"So, you're forty, pal. You are forty!" Then he laughed. "Welcome to middle age." He slapped my shoulder. I ate my cake with no enthusiasm.

So the "Year of Mourning the Loss of My Youth" was officially launched. And was I depressed.

Later that year a national magazine ran a special feature on people who had made it *before* forty. I wasn't included nor was anyone that I knew personally. So, I really clamped down professionally. Just a few months left to make it *before* the mystic Four-0. Repeatedly I heard that line from the invitational "Softly and Tenderly:" "Time is now fleeting, the moments are passing."

It was time to go on the offensive.

TAKE CHARGE!

My father had a saying that I heard frequently as a child, "Well, don't just sit there like a bump on a log. Do something!"

The message got through. Trained as a researcher, I decided to draft a questionnaire to send to friends and associates asking for their perspectives and advice. I wrote:

On August 21 I will be experiencing my fortieth birthday. As something of a milestone, it seems to be time to give some serious thought to the next ten years of my life and career. But it also seems a good time to tinker, to fine-tune, and to take a good hard look at what it means to me to be forty years old.

We've been friends for some time now. That's why I feel free to ask a favor of you. Could you take some time, in the next couple of weeks, to give some advice to me? From your vantage point, what are my strengths? What are my weaknesses? How could our friendship be improved? Where do you think I should invest my energies? If you could help me see one thing about myself that has frustrated or concerned you, what would that be?

Once the letter was drafted, I next pondered my address book. To whom should I send the letter? I wanted real reactions, so I chose people who would be honest — in a few cases, brutally honest.

Since they were busy people, I made the questionnaire simple. On the right side I asked them to list five strengths of mine, on the left side, five weaknesses.

Then I asked two questions and left space for them to respond:

(1) How could our friendship be strengthened?
(2) Where should I invest my energies in the next ten years?

Finally, I asked for, "Your advice to me about turning forty."

Needless to say, the last thirty days of my thirty-ninth year

brought plenty of mail. Some of the responses included:
- "Is this for real?"
- "I wish I had had this idea when I turned forty."
- "You certainly are an open-minded person to request information about yourself."
- "It meant a lot to me that you would ask me to respond to your questionnaire."
- "Happy birthday. I think this is a wild idea, but here it goes. . . . "
- "Hey! What's this I hear of you getting down because you're turning 'forty.' Huh? You are approaching this whole thing a little bit 'off.' "

Many sent cards with words of encouragement. Many, who had tuned forty before me—offered some rich advice from their experience. As Bill Ratliff has written, "Sometimes the affirmations of those who have emerged from the shadows of doubt and struggle can provide a trust fund from which we can borrow until we have 'trust funds' of our own."[1] Several times I have turned back to the questionnaires for another reading. I have treasured their words to this day, when I sometimes ask, "What was that fuss all about, anyway?"

I have concluded that *turning* forty is more difficult than *being* forty.

The Sunday after my birthday, I attended a congregation that used the lectionary in their worship services. I was stunned by the opening passage from Jeremiah 15:15: "Oh Lord, Thou knowest; remember me and visit me" (RSV).

And the epistle that morning was another reminder: "I appeal to you therefore, brethren, by the mercies of God, to present your bodies as a living sacrifice, holy and acceptable to God, which is your spiritual worship. Do not be conformed to this world but be transformed by the renewal of your mind, that you may prove what is the will of God, what is good and acceptable and perfect" (Rom. 12:1-2, RSV).

I remembered that day that regardless of our age God knows, God remembers, and God cares.

I was reminded that regardless of candles on the cake, that the task is always the same: to present, to renew, to prove the will of God. Each birthday calls for a reexamination.

Enough about *turning* forty; let's shift our attention to *being* fortysomething. Do you remember the Old Testament story about the sun standing still? Joshua was leading the Israelites into battle against the Amorites. And Joshua — known to have no problems with boldness — prayed, "O sun, stand still over Gideon, O moon, over the Valley of Aijalon" (Josh. 10:12). One bold prayer. Well, the forties are a time, believe me, for equally bold prayers.

Scripture says, "The sun stopped in the middle of the sky and delayed going down about a full day. There has never been a day like it before or since, a day when the Lord listened to a man" (Josh. 10:13-14).

HOW ARE YOU GOING TO USE THE DECADE?

Forty is the beginning of a new decade: at least, 3,652 days (remember you get at least two, perhaps three extra days, for leap years) lie ahead. It is also a time for questions. The most basic may well be: *Do I want to live the rest of my life the way I have lived my life so far?* Or as one forty-eight-year-old phrased it, "Is there another way to lead a good life?"[2]

Consider this quotation from the poet Rilke:

I want to beg you, as much as I can, to be patient toward all that is unresolved in your heart; try to love the questions themselves like locked rooms or books that are written in a foreign tongue. Do not now seek the answers; they cannot be given to you because you would not be able to live them. And the point is to live everything. Live the questions now. You will then gradually, without even noticing it perhaps, live along some day into the answer.[3]

Let me offer some goals that will help us "live" into the answer.

Goal #1: To Admit That I Am Forty Years Old and (Still) Single. For some of us, it is no problem admitting that we are forty (our evasive answers will start next decade).

The real issue may be: But I didn't think I would be single. Or *still* single. This is one reason a single adult's frustration over turning forty is different than a married adult's.

Many of us still have well-rehearsed romantic fantasies. Prince Charming will appear and carry us off on the back of a white charger . . . or the fairy-tale princess will lead us into the land of ooohhh's and aaahhh's commonly called marriage.

We wonder if he/she will ever get here. This is particularly compounded when parents want grandchildren. The situation may become more difficult if you are the only hope: The family name ends unless you do your part *soon*.

For single women, this makes turning forty even more difficult. As a male I am potentially reproductive for most of my life. This is not so for a woman. She may feel caught between a clock and a hard place. I discovered that as I sat at dinner with a very attractive woman. She had it all: tremendous job, great salary, friends, creativity, wit. Yet, she had not married.

I listened as she talked about her "ungrieved" grief. I had no words to offer. No rebuttals. No well-meaning, "Yes but's."

Some fortysomethings panic and buy into the advice of one of the fad books, on "how to meet and marry a man/woman in thirty days." Tragically, others at this juncture, angrily snarl, "God, I gave you time. Now I'm in charge."

Perhaps you heard about the forty-year-old bride. When the minister asked, "Do you take this man to be your lawfully wedded husband, to have and to hold from this day forward?" she snapped with a shrug, "He'll do!" That happens too often.

Some single adults have said, "Forget love. I want to be married!" My good friend Jim Town placed this mindset into perspective with his observation: "The only thing worse than not having what you want . . . is having something you don't want!"

Goal #2: To Assess the Past. A counselor friend of mine asks what I call a "killer" question of his clients: "What are you pretending *not* to know?"

Too many single adults in their forties have not come to terms with their pasts. There is still unfinished business littering their pasts. Most of this has to do with relationships: friends, "ex's," parents, siblings.

For some it is simple: "*If* he/she had married me *then*, I would not be single now." The issue is compounded when your social circle bumps against your former "friend's" social circle and he/she now has the perfect American family: 2.3 kids, PTA membership, suburban house with a picket fence and landscaped yard, and sender of Christmas photocards. And you're *still* in the single adult department (which may be very difficult for your mother to include in the family Christmas letter).

The past is finished. We must not try to make it the present or future. By continuing to hold on to the past, you could be keeping your hands so full you can't reach out to embrace the present.

Goal #3: To Position Yourself for the Future. The future belongs to those who plan for it, and not just those who want a future.

How many of us have had parents say, "Think about your future. You're not getting any younger." In essence they are saying, singleness is OK now but what about down the road? And usually the questioner lowers his or her voice to emphasize those last words: *down the road* — when you are fifty . . . sixty . . . seventy! In the anxiety of being forty, one's thinking can become muddled. No one has addressed this issue more clearly, than Amy Carmichael.

Profile of a Fortysomething: Amy Carmichael (1867–1951). Author, missionary, founder of the Dohnavur Fellowship. First went to Japan as a missionary in 1893; due to ill health served in Ceylon and England. In 1895 established a home for children in Dohnavur, India, under the auspices of the Church of England Zenana Missionary Society. Because her heart went out to young girls involved in Hindu worship, Amy organized the Dohnavur Fellowship in 1927. Her many books include *If.* She once wrote:

On this day many years ago I went away alone to a cave in a mountain called Arima. I had feelings of fear about the future, that was why I went there—to be alone with God. The devil kept whispering, "It's all right now, but what about afterwards? You are going to be very lonely." And he painted pictures of my loneliness—I can see them still. And I turned to God in a kind of desperation and said, "Lord, what can I do? How can I go on to the end?" and He said, "None of them that trust in Me shall be desolate." That word has been with me ever since. It has been fulfilled to me. It will be fulfilled to you.[4]

We may run out of future. That's why we must live abundantly now—today.

Dag Hammarskjold, a single male, served from 1953 to 1961 as Secretary General of the United Nations. During his career as a diplomat he kept a diary of his faith. After his death, the diary was found and published as *Markings.* He wrote, "For all that has been—thanks. For all that is to be—yes." He did not realize that that "yes" would mean death in Africa as he tried to stop a war in what had been the Belgian Congo. His greatest honor would come posthumously, the 1961 Nobel Peace Prize.[5]

I have a missionary friend, Elisabeth, who faithfully served God in Africa. She ended an engagement to go; she experienced the death of her parents and a brother while there. Then, in her pre-retirement planning, Elisabeth began dreading returning to the United States. Africa was her home, but under missionary board policy she had to return to this country.

In retirement Elizabeth renewed an acquaintance with a former colleague, who had retired and had been widowed. You can guess the end of the story—they married.

Why? Because she positioned herself for the future by not being bitter over her singleness. I've never forgotten the smile on her face when she said of marriage, "What a delicious surprise—all those years God had this waiting for me."

Goal #4: To Reexamine My Dreams. By this stage of our lives, some of us have a string of collapsed dreams, failures, injustices. Events without "they lived happily ever after" endings.

Like Jacob who in his forties encountered the Lord, some of us now walk with a limp. But we also walk with a blessing.

The forties are a great time to take an inventory of our dreams. Sometimes I have wondered what my life would have been like *if* I had become a minister of music (which was once a goal); or *if* I had become a missionary (another dream).

But I never dreamed of being a writer. I never thought of having a ministry with single adults that would take me all over the globe. As a fortysomething, are you "open" to life's surprises?

Sometimes we need a "dreamsort." I'll keep this . . . I'll get rid of this. It is never too late to make a dream come true. Your dream deserves a chance. A *renewed* yes.

Goal #5: To Question My Priorities and Commitments. What is at the Center of My Life? That's the midlife issue for most of us. What is at the center of your life? A dream? A fantasy? A nightmare? An ache? A memory? A person? God? Yourself? Sadly, some of us cannot even put it into words.

Maybe it is a caustic declaration from a parent, three or four decades ago: "You'll never amount to anything!"

Or maybe it was another's observation, "You're just like your father! What a waste!"

In school for a history test, you probably memorized a single adult's battle cry. Once his ship had been heavily damaged, the British commander demanded that the American naval officer surrender. But John Paul Jones declared, "I have not yet begun to fight!" He won that battle and a slew of others and became an American hero.

In his forties, Jones became a commodore in the Russian Navy. He possessed tremendous integrity. On one occasion, when Jones realized that the government would not pay his sailors as much as overzealous recruiters had promised, he paid the difference out of his own pocket.

Though thought of as a hero, John Paul Jones had a past. In fact his legal name was John Paul. He had first gone to sea at age twelve and had commanded his first ship at twenty-two. But, on a cruise in the East Indies, he had put down a mutiny and "killed" a man. After this incident, John Paul came to America incognito and added "Jones" to his name.

At the time the American Revolution broke out he was a drifter, relying on the generosity of strangers. Through friendships with leading members of the Continental Congress he won his first American command.

I have long wondered what made this single adult a hero. Any navy, in those days, was a pretty "wild" scene for seafaring men. One biographer noted of Jones:

> He had no fondness for revelry, jolly coffee-house dinner, or drinking bouts, which formed the principal amusements in foreign ports. While others were carousing ashore he was studying in his cabin, perfecting himself in history and languages, pondering upon the maneuvering of ships and the grand strategy of navel warfare, and *paving the way for his future victories, which were won first with the brain then with the sword.*[6] (emphasis mine)

What about you? As a forty-year-old, are you paving the way for future victories? Or rehashing lost ones of the twenties and thirties? Are you out "carousing" with the gang or in your cabin-equivalent preparing for the future?

These days, I am rigorously reexamining the yeses of my life. Someone has said, "Your yeses mean nothing, until your nos mean something." I've said yes to one too many invitations, one too many books, and one too many desserts.

The good news is that I don't have to live the rest of my

life like the first half. And neither do you. These days called the forties can be a time-out, a breathing space.

I am free to take my tickets and see what other rides are available in this amusement park called fortyland — some of which I have never tried because I have gotten used to or comfortable on the merry-go-round.

CONCLUSION

Your fourth decade can be a valuable period of growth. First, however, you must admit that you are forty and single — none of this "thirty-nine and holding" business. You must assess the past. Some single adults allow the past too much influence in their lives. You must position yourself for a great future that can be yours regardless of the past. You must reexamine your dreams. It's never too late to dust off a dream. Finally, by admitting that you are forty *and* single, you can reexamine your priorities and commitments. You can make yourself open to life's surprises.

QUESTIONS

1. In what ways do you admit or deny that you are a forty-something?
2. Would you feel comfortable asking friends to complete the profile on page 153? Take a moment and list the friends you would ask.
3. Are you more concerned that you are still single or single-again or that you are forty?
4. Do you want to live the rest of your life as a rerun of the first three decades? List the immediate decisions you would have to make to live a better life. Then list the long-range decisions.
5. Reflect again on Dag Hammarskjold's words: "For all that has been — thanks. For all that is to be — yes." To what extent can you agree? Was he being idealistic?
6. What choices can you make in the next few weeks to pave the way for future victories?
7. Think back over the previous forty years. Now list what you have said "yes" and "no" to.

C h a p t e r   T w o

EVERY DAY...
IN EVERY WAY...
I'M GETTING OLDER

*Those of us in mid-life today are at the heart
of a major redefinition of "middle age"...
for those who follow us ... the middle
years will be fundamentally transformed.
What has been a dreaded and shunned phase
of life
will become for them a highly valued and
productive time.*
•   *— Jane Fonda*

GOAL FOR FORTYSOMETHINGS: To admit that I
am getting older.

This past Easter, as I was driving to brunch a sign captured
my attention beside the road: "Diane Turner has only 365
days until she turns 40!" While I don't know Diane and am
not certain how she reacted to the announcement, I am certain that some visitors to Kansas City—particularly from other
cultures—would be confused by the sign.

The sign illustrates the power of contemporary American
attitudes on aging. It also underscores a central truth: Diane
can do nothing about the reality of growing older. But she can
determine her response to aging. Like adolescence, Diane,
and millions of us fortysomethings, will have to navigate this
"turning point." Who taught us to be a teenager? No one. We
learned by *being* a teen. So it will be with mid-life. We will
learn by being fortysomething.

The entry into mid-life has five dimensions—not unlike those of death: (1) *Denial*—Not me! (2) *Anger*—Why me? Answer: because your birth certificate says so. (3) *Bargaining*— I'll lose weight . . . I'll work out . . . (4) *Depression*—I'm losing my attractiveness . . . my youth, and (5) *Acceptance*—This is an opportunity, not a problem!

WHEN DOES MID-LIFE BEGIN?

Perhaps you saw the touching movie *On Golden Pond* starring Henry Fonda and Katherine Hepburn. One wonderful exchange took place between Norman Thayer (Fonda) and his wife Ethel (Hepburn) when she tried to convince him that they were *older* but not old.

> Norman: Middle age means middle, Ethel, the middle of life. People don't live to be a hundred and fifty.
> Ethel: We are at the far edge of middle age, that's all.
> Norman: We're not, you know. We're not middle-aged. You're old and I'm ancient.
> Ethel: Oh, pooh. You're in your seventies and I'm in my sixties.
> Norman: Just barely, on both counts.[1]

Science and good nutrition have helped redefine the term *mid-life*. In 1900, life expectancy at birth was 47.3 years for both sexes. Simply, not enough people lived long enough to make mid-life so definable. A half century later expectancy was 68.2 years; by 1985, it had reached 74.7 years.[2]

We cannot define the exact age at which mid-life begins. For example, immediately after saying, "I am fifty," many will quickly add, "But I feel forty." Few adults, these days, want to act their age. Moreover, Robert Maxwell, a spokesman for the American Association of Retired Persons observed, "Our society is getting older, but the old are getting younger."[3]

Daniel J. Levinson, regarded as the expert on mid-life, in his classic, *The Seasons of a Man's Life*, discussed life's predictable stages. I have included the following schematic drawing, adapted from Levinson, to explain his thinking:[4]

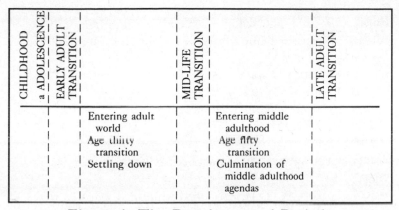

Figure 1: The Developmental Periods

Clearly, the above is only a guide. There is a great deal of overlap, particularly between early and middle adulthood, and between middle and late adulthood. No doubt this trend will continue as the numbers of single adults marrying later increases. For example, my mother married at sixteen and had a first child at seventeen; my sister married at fifteen and had a son at sixteen. So, my mother was a grandmother at thirty-three! I am forty-two and still unmarried. Even if I married now and had a child, at the age by which my mother had several grandchildren, I would just be becoming a father.

Gunhild Hagestad, a specialist in human development, noted, "Adults in the family now confront each other in relationships for which there is no historical precedence and minimal cultural guidance, while they individually find themselves in life stages that also have few culturally shared expectations attached to them."[5]

This is even more complicated by men who divorce, marry a younger woman, and begin a second family, so that stepbrothers and sisters are a full generation apart. Family relationships, these days, are characterized by interesting combinations of siblings and rivalries.

One of the earliest development psychologists, Robert J. Havinghurst, formulated what he labeled "the developmental tasks of adulthood." In an earlier book, *Positively Single* (Victor Books, 1983), I analyzed his theory as it applied to single adults. His tasks included:

1. Selecting a mate.
2. Learning to live with a mate.
3. Starting a family.
4. Rearing children.
5. Managing a home.
6. Getting started in an occupation.
7. Taking on civic responsibility.
8. Finding a congenial social group.[6]

Most of these apply to adults in their twenties. Naturally though, in today's singles world, one can find exceptions: single adults who are launching a new career or a new family at forty-five rather than at twenty-five.

Middle adults, according to Havinghurst must:

1. *Assist* teenage children to become responsible and happy adults (a difficult task—particularly when so many are "renesting" or returning home).
2. *Achieve* adult social and civic responsibility.
3. *Reach* and *maintain* satisfactory performance in a career.
4. *Develop* adult leisure activities.
5. *Relate* to one's spouse as a person.
6. *Accept* and adjust to physiological changes.
7. *Adjust* to aging parents.[7]

LEARNING FROM RESEARCH

Let's examine some individuals who have been the significant researchers on mid-life.

Erik Erikson. Many would consider Erickson to be the key theoretician of adult development. He offered an "ages and stages" approach, identifying eight stages of growth from birth to the grave. The first seven stages involved "doing" or completing a particular task so that a person could move on to the next stage. Erikson's two major tasks for middle adults are generativity and individuation.

(1) *Generativity:* attempts to resolve the conflict between absorption with the self and the need to help others via parenting, teaching, volunteering—the major task is guiding the next generation.

(2) *Individuation:* tries to come to terms with the "shadows" of one's personality that have not heretofore been dealt with. This may be a time to renegotiate the boundaries between self and the world. During this period, many single adults will struggle with a powerful need for attachment to others and paradoxically an important need for separateness.

Many assume that Erikson's work is carved in granite. Not so, argued Jerry Gerber and others in *Life-trends.* They dismiss his theory based on research in the 1940s and 1950s as outdated because of the degree of social change in the family, work world and culture.[8]

Bernice Neugarten contends that changing times and different social expectations affect how various groups or "cohorts" (groups of people born in the same year or same time period) experience mid-life. "Our values are shaped by the period in which we live." Kent State, Vietnam, Watergate have significantly impacted the worldview and internal view of many boomers. "The social environment of a particular age group can influence its social clock—the timetable [a la Havinghurst] when people expect and are expected to accomplish some of the major tasks of adult life."[9]

Gail Sheehy. Five million copies of Sheehy's book, *Passages* made the phrase "mid-life crisis" a household expression. One friend who found her husband reading the book snapped, "Just because that books says you are supposed to have one, doesn't mean that you are!" *Passages* was based on the research of stage-theorist scholars who mainly studied men. Sociologist Orville Brim dismissed Sheehy's formulistic approach and comfortable answers as "a little like horoscopes. They are vague enough so that everyone can see something of themselves in them."[10]

Moreover, Sheehy relied heavily on research by Roger Gould who has since restated his theories. He now rejects the idea that there are structured, well-defined stages or an itinerary of tasks to be mastered. Gould admits that people do "change their ways of looking at and experiencing the world over time." However, the notion that you have to complete one stage in order to tackle the next is "hogwash."[11]

Gould suggests that adults must modify their early expectations as they age. "Childhood delivers more people into adulthood with a view of adults that few could ever live up to. Adults must confront this impossible image or be frustrated and dissatisfied."[12]

Simply, today's single adult baby boomers and their married boomer friends, will force many of the experts to redraft their theories. This generation has little interest in doing anything "by the book."![13]

Daniel J. Levinson. The most illuminating of the male mid-life research was conducted by Yale psychologist Levinson in the late 1960s. He studied forty men, between the ages of thirty-five and forty-five and developed a comprehensive framework of developmental stages. Levinson concluded:

(1) The mid-life is a predictable stage of development that *all* men [and women] go through.
(2) For *some*, the transition may go smoothly, while for others it involves considerable disruption.
(3) For many, mid-life is marked by confusion and introspection.
(4) The mid-life is not only predictable but also desirable because it offers opportunities for new personality growth and life changes, never before possible, particularly in today's socio-economic climate.
(5) The mid-life profoundly impacts one's future.[14]

Daniel Levinson has dismissed the label, "mid-life crisis" as a pop term or catchall. He preferred the term *transition,* which implies the individual has more control. "It is the bridge from early to middle adulthood, and its main characteristic is change: ending one life structure and beginning another."[15]

Levinson suggests that adulthood is composed of three overlapping stages of roughly twenty-five years each:

- Early adulthood: 17-45
- Middle adulthood: 40-65
- Late adulthood: 60-?[16]

These chunks of time have physiological, psychological, and philosophical dimensions.

THE PHYSIOLOGICAL REALITIES
The psalmist said, "I praise You because I am fearfully and wonderfully made" (Ps. 139:14). Some of us might counter that he knew little about sags, wrinkles, bulges, and pot-bellies. He also said, "My frame was not hidden from You when I was made in the secret place" (v. 15), nor is our current frame. Rachel Dulin, in *A Biblical View of Aging*, points out that the biblical writers were aware of aging. Ezekiel and the psalmists "observed" three periods: childhood, youth, and old age (Ps. 148:12; Ezek. 9:6); Jeremiah saw four: childhood, youth, adulthood, and old age (Jer. 6:11; 51:22). Certainly, the writers of Scripture saw a difference between being an older person and being "blessed" with a prolonged life.[17] Thus, Abraham "died at a good old age, an old man and full of years" (Gen. 25:8).

The biblical writers reported the physical changes: graying; loss of eyesight; loss of hearing; loss of potency; inability to enjoy the sex act; physiological inability to impregnate or to conceive; loss of strength; and loss of taste.[18]

Let's look at some of our physiological changes:

- Skin loses elasticity—more easily bruised; dryer; healing takes more time.
- Hair for men either grays or recedes; women may notice more facial hair.
- Bone mass decreases.
- Muscle mass may decrease based on amount of exercise.
- Joints stiffen and muscles lose resiliency; connective tis-

sue loses flexibility, becomes weaker, and loses water.
- Physical endurance declines; some decline in dexterity.
- Decrease in gastric secretions.
- Cardiovascular changes; hardening of heart muscle; decreased rhythm and tone for those with sedentary lifestyle.
- Menopause leads to degenerative changes in ovaries.
- Increase in body fat distribution around abdomen and hips.
- Tendency toward farsightedness.
- Gradual slowing of reactions.
- Gradual loss of hearing, especially high tones for males.
- Brain cell loss begins.[19]

Of course these changes are impacted by the condition of the body you brought to mid-life. Crash dieting, poor nutrition, and lack of exercise will impact these changes significantly.

Fortysomethings also burn fewer calories. One researcher notes, "If you continue to consume the same number of calories (you did as a young adult), those not burned will turn to fat. For instance, if you eat just 100 calories more than you use up every day, you can expect to gain more than fifty pounds in five years."[20] Tell me that isn't so! Think about that at the next singles' potluck. Those locked in the fast lane of the fast-food express pay a big price for their fuel.[21]

Let's take a moment and protest responsively: "IT ISN'T FAIR!"

Genetics also has a role to play. Some of us are seemingly predisposed to fighting the weight gain and gravity battle more than others. For some it will be a battle over distribution. You may still weigh the same but find you cannot wear (and breathe at the same time) the waist size that you have worn for years.

Instead of "Get thee to a nunnery!" the new injunction is "Get thee to a health club!" No wonder, so many single adults are finding health clubs the new place to meet the opposite sex.

This means that most fortysomethings need a serious exposure to the word *discipline.*

In my own life, I can testify to attempting to "eat" my way through my mid-life crisis. My eating habits resulted in an awkward conversation with my physician: "Let's see, in 1987 you weighed . . . and now you weigh thirty-five pounds more." Worst of all, I had to pay for his amazing mathematical calculations.

After some annoyance and irritation, I have accepted responsibility for this aging "temple." From this point on it's patch and maintain.

Of course, the pivotal event for fortysomething females is menopause. This is the significant gender difference in the way mid-life is perceived and experienced. Traditionally, menopause has been used as a blanket explanation for women in middle adulthood. We've all heard whispered comments like, "You know, *the change of life.*"

Researchers are now reexamining the physiological impact of menopause. Kaluger and Kaluger note, "every period of life, from childhood to old age, has its joys and trials." This period, too, has its compensations. The word menopause comes from the Greek words "month' and "cessation."

Symptoms begin with major hormonal changes between the ages of forty and fifty-five. In one major study, only 3.5 percent of the cases occurred before age forty and 31.5 percent after age fifty.[22]

The symptoms include a reduction of the influence of the ovaries, which in turn, affects other glands and systems in the female. Some women notice a general slowing down of the monthly menses; others experience an abrupt cessation.

Many physiologists say that there is no such thing as a male menopause. While there is no physical change comparable to that experienced by females, male attitudes on sex and sexual performance patterns may change during this period; although this is seldom a result of a hormonal decline. Fatigue and stress are cited as primary causes for this decrease in sexual activity and desire.

Some argue that any male sexual changes are a self-fulfilling prophecy. If fortysomething males do not want to be middle-aged, they may find themselves battling the hormones and engaging in bizarre sexual conduct to shore up their fragile masculine egos. This may be particularly true among the mid-life recently divorced, particularly if the male feels, "dumped." The Kalugers conclude that in 1 percent of males there is a period in which the reproductive powers decrease, but that this is due to primary testicular failure.[23]

THE PSYCHOLOGICAL REALITIES

Between ages twenty and thirty the sexual capacity and drives are at their peak. After that point, due to work responsibility and/or parenting, some experience a decisive decline in sexual drives and behaviors.

Anne Morrow Lindbergh wrote, "But in middle age, because of the false assumption that it is a period of decline, one interprets these life-signs, paradoxically, as signs of approaching death. Instead of facing them, one runs away; one escapes—into depressions, nervous breakdowns, drink, love affairs, or frantic, thoughtless, fruitless overwork. Anything, rather than face them. One tries to cure the signs of growth, to exorcise them, as if they were devils, when really they might be angels of annunciation."[24]

The Pennsylvania Dutch have a proverb, "Throw the horse over the fence some hay." This awkward grammar does not make much sense. The Kalugers say that mid-life can be equally awkward. "Ve get too soon oldt, und too late schmart."[25] So, in a few years some of us will be saying, if only I had known *then* what I know now.[25]

Joseph Bailey describing neo-cognitive psychology, convincingly argues that thought creates our psychological experience and no doubt some of our physiological experiences and expressions as well. Good thoughts, he argues, lead to good experiences and lifestyles. This concept squares with the proverbialist's observation, "For as he thinketh in his heart, so is he" (Prov. 23:7, KJV).

Bailey has developed "a cycle of stress" that works as described below. First, consider the notion: I am old!

Stage 1:   THOUGHT SEEN AS REAL: Fortysomething loses the conscious awareness that a thought (I am old!) is not necessarily the truth.

Stage 2:   INSECURITY: Fortysomething takes the thought and adds her insecurities to it: "I am old and therefore unattractive" which validates her emotions and stress.

Stage 3:   FOCUSING ON DETAILS: Fortysomething develops a preoccupation with the original thought.

Stage 4:   TRIGGERS HABITS: The thoughts trigger habit patterns to deal with stressful thoughts: anger, depression, withdrawal, panic.

Stage 5:   SITUATION WORSENS: Fortysomething experiences more stress (teasing when people see how sensitive he is about his age).

Stage 5:   THOUGHT VALIDATED: Teasing, brooding, misconstruing responses only validate the initial thought.

Stage 7:   BURNOUT: Stress, depression, anxiety increasingly become part of fortysomething's day.

Stage 8:   THOUGHT NOW BELIEVED AS REAL. This is a vicious cycle influenced by the concept of self-fulfilling prophecy. If I feed my mind enough "bad" data, I begin to believe it. Suddenly, I have aches and pains to accompany the expectations of aches and pains: I have them because I am supposed to have them.[26]

Robert Kastenbaum calls this a "developmental crisis" because it is a threatening situation confronted at a certain time in one's lifespan.[27] Moreover, mid-life can be heightened by stress-packed scenarios. Consider the following crises:

• *Children leaving home:* Many fortysomethings react adversely to the empty nest. "But I am not old enough to have a son in college, a daughter getting married, or be a grandparent!" If a couple has poured their energies into raising their children, what do they do when the children leave the nest? This may be even more acutely felt by single parents whose children have become the center of their lives.

• *Mid-life affairs:* There is a correlation between divorce and mid-life. That often prompts the question, "What's getting into all these people?" Indeed, we see this pattern frequently: Husband meets woman at work; husband gets involved with woman; husband leaves wife for the other woman; husband divorces wife and marries woman at work.

Admittedly, many men are looking for a new taste of sexual excitement to replace the boredom that may have developed in their marriages. The enormous infusion of young women into the workplace has created a captive audience. A man's level of achievement at mid-life may make him attractive to women in a way that he is not to his spouse. After all, he has power, prestige, and success—a trinity of aphrodisiacs. Nancy Mayer says of men, "the young woman can enhance your ego by reflecting back on you the image you want to have reflected."[28] Sexual affairs make the man feel not only potent but often omnipotent.

Sexual functional changes frighten many. Men in mid-life take longer than in the past to achieve an erection. The force of his orgasm may be less intense and satisfying. Because of the pressure put on a man to sexually "perform," the first time he cannot achieve an erection can be a life-changing moment if he misdefines his sexuality as do so many American males: I am as I perform! Sadly, even in the evangelical world, many males have been taught to value performance over pleasure and to detach sexuality from their souls. Males who continue to regard sex as "genital combat" will be grief-stricken by the physical changes.

Realistically, not all single adult males are celibate. Many coming out of a divorce—particularly when sexual relations were poor—will have a fear or curiosity about their sexual abilities, as well as a sense of competition with younger males that lead to sexual struggles, experimentation, and scars. Some use sex as an anesthetic for their psychological pain.[29]

●*Fatigue:* Many single adults in mid-life are physically tired from routines and responsibilities, especially if they admire the lifestyle and freedom of single adults who are not parents. Some singles feel squeezed by responsibility for aging parents as well as their own children.

● *Work crisis:* Despite age discrimination laws, the corporate world does not ignore birthdays. If a fortysomething finds himself out of a job, he may have great difficulty getting another at comparable pay and status. Moreover, spending a number of years with one company may now be perceived in a negative light; loyalists are suspect. In the age of buy outs, many fortysomethings have found themselves on the street, résumé in hand, competing with recent college graduates.

The results of one ten-year University of Chicago study of aging (of more than 700 men and women) disclosed attributes or characteristics that related to the psychological adjustment and mental health. Emotionally healthy fortysomethings had these things in common:

(1) *Emotional flexibility:* the capacity to shift emotional investments from one person to another. A lot of single adults have too many people demanding things and attention from them.

(2) *Mental flexibility:* the capacity to use experience as a provisional guide rather than as a fixed point of refer ence. Fortysomethings can learn new tricks.

(3) *Ego differentiation:* the capacity to pursue and to enjoy a varied set of major activities without relying too extensively on one or two roles.

(4) *Body transcendence:* the capacity to feel happy and avoid preoccupation with health, physique, and bodily comfort. The ability to say, "This is me at mid-life!"

(5) *Ego transcendence:* the capacity to be involved in a manner in which one reacts with concern for the well-being of others. The ability to avoid preoccupation with the mid-life transition.

(6) *Sexual integration:* the capacity to mesh one's sexual desires and longings with other aspects and responsibilities of life. Such an individual is not hormone-driven or
hormone-centered.

The researchers concluded, "Personality adjustment in the
middle years appears to be related to the individual's capacity
to properly utilize these . . . characteristics."[31]

The results of these studies can be summarized simply:
When life bestows a lemon, healthy fortysomethings have the
ability, persistence, and willingness to make lemonade.

THE PHILOSOPHICAL REALITIES

Mid-life is either a crisis or a transition, and one's philosophical moorings influence the direction.

The psalmist wrote, "Trust in the Lord and do good; dwell
in the land and enjoy safe pasture. Delight yourself in the
Lord and He will give you the desires of your heart" (Ps. 37:3-
4). Too many of us don't trust the desires of our heart or
don't have the slightest inkling of what lasting desires are or
should be.

By mid-life, according to Levinson, the fortysomething
should have made a place for self in the adult world and have
created a life structure that will be visible in the world and
suitable for the nourishment of that self.[32]

Some fortysomethings groan, "I wish."

For many, the great philosophical questions begin lining up
to interrupt the thoughts of the once young professional scam-
pering up the ladder of success:

- Who am I?
- What have I done with my life?
- What have I gotten out of life?
- What have I given to life?
- What is it that I truly want?
- Is it possible for me to reach my potential?
- Is this really what I want?
- Is this worth it?

Such questions lead fortysomethings to four agendas:

- To reappraise commitments.
- To explore alternatives.
- To test options.
- To maintain this life or to create a new one.[33]

It is as if someone is now aware that the timer is ticking. Elliot Jaques declares, "The central issue at mid-life is coming to terms with one's own mortality: as man must learn now, more deeply than was possible before, that his own death is inevitable and that he and others are capable of great destructiveness."[34] Indeed, fears of death will fuel his work on the agendas.

During this sensitive time distress can be heightened by the premature death of a friend, colleague, business partner, or relative, particularly if by heart attack.

The refrain, *Is that all there is?* begins to resound through the canyons of the spirit. For some it becomes a *now* or *never* opportunity. They feel that this could be the last chance to realize unfulfilled dreams. Suddenly, not only may one have failed to "make it" or reach his or her potential; now the word *never* has a new sound to it. Sadly, at this point some fortysomethings seek for and find someone to blame: parents, a spouse, or the mysterious "they."

Levinson reminds us that "to understand a man's life, therefore, we must take into account the society in which he lives."[35] What if the fortysomething has not married? Levinson says, "In all societies, a man is expected to marry and to take certain responsibilities within a familial system."[36] That is even more true in evangelical or fundamentalist Christian subcultures where singleness after thirty is either viewed suspiciously or as a tragedy.

Simply, the absence of marriage may increase mid-life anxiety. Some fortysomethings don't just want to get married, they *need* to be married to consider themselves whole and successful. Some argue that marriage will resolve their strained emotional state, not realizing that the loneliest person in their zip code is not a single adult but rather a married fortysomething, saying, "If only I were single. . . . "

For some the failure of a marriage or an unwanted divorce has made them emotional adult orphans. They wander across "Singleland" like emotional refugees or displaced persons, grasping at emotional straws.

Almost anyone in mid-life has at one time or another felt like the Jews in the Babylonian Captivity. "How shall we sing the Lord's song in a strange land?" (Ps. 137:4, kjv) Mid-life is a psychological "strange land" — not unlike a type of time-out. And for some fortysomethings the most terrifying question is: How shall I sing the Lord's song if I never marry, remarry, or have children?

CONCLUSION

Every day, in every way, you are getting older. Of course, older is relative to one's attitudes, health, and philosophy of life. The mid-life can be a welcomed experience for the spiritually and psychologically healthy single adult.

As single adults we need to befriend the physiological changes rather than waste so much time fighting the body. Indeed, how I feel about these changes will be more important than the changes themselves.

The task of these years is to remodel our life structure. The task requires lots of thought, prayer, and guidance to make those key choices that will enable our structure to stand against the "storms" of mid-life.[37]

QUESTIONS

1. What are your fears about turning/being forty? How are you facing them?
2. What are the myths about being forty that you have heard?
3. When did middle-age begin for you? Was it a particular event? If so, what made that event a turning point?
4. Are you in mid-life transition or crisis?
5. What body changes trouble you most?
6. What is fueling your discontent about getting older?

THERE'S MORE TO BEING FORTY AND SINGLE THAN WAITING FOR THE RIGHT ONE TO SHOW UP

*I broke the back of life yesterday and started
downhill toward old age. This fact
has not produced any effect on me
that I can detect.*
— *Mark Twain, written on 43rd birthday*

GOAL FOR FORTYSOMETHINGS: To develop a
healthy perspective on singleness and being forty.

Picture this: An impatient bride stands in front of a large
grandfather clock, scowling. Impatiently she taps her toes.
"He had better have a good excuse for where he has been all
this time!" she fumes.

That's true of many fortysomethings. We're waiting — tired
of waiting for the charming prince or princess to show up. For
too many, life is on hold until the "I do" moment. But the
truth is for many of us there will be no I do moment, that is,
not in the traditional wedding sense. Hopefully we will experience another moment when we say I do and *accept* being
forty and single.

All of us respond to being forty and single through our
unique experiences, hopes, desires, and longings. For some
this stage of life is "no sweat." For others, it is a major

emotional crisis. "I cannot believe that I am *still* single," say some. Others can verbalize no more than an anguished "Why?" directed to God, parents, dates, counselors, or anyone who will listen.

The way we view our situation is shaped by our parents, our educations, our temperaments, and our religious commitments. For example, if you grew up in a religious tradition that constantly emphasized, "Girls, be true. God has someone for you," by this time that message has grown a little thin. Cultural climate is a significant influence. Alice Rossi contends that Baby Boomers will experience a different mid-life than say, depression-born individuals. "Baby boomers have different dreams, values and opportunities than the preceding generations. And they are more numerous."[1] Boomers are far better educated and healthier than previous generations who have faced mid-life.

If you grew up with parents that were uncomfortable with singleness—particularly *your* singleness—this fortysomething season of your life takes on a different meaning than for a single with a supportive family.

If you have longed to be married, you will perceive this reality differently than someone who is only mildly disappointed or inconvenienced by the wait.

If you have been exposed to positive models of mature singleness, then you accept the reality differently.

Some single adults have literally taken the words of Jesus to "seek first His Kingdom" (Matt. 6:33) and have faced mid-life based on that. General Eva Burrows, head of the worldwide Salvation Army, acknowledged that being a "salvationist" was foremost on her mind in college (when many women were thinking about romance) as well as in her forties.

I was very much dedicated to the purpose God had for me. Possibly some of the men might have been a little intimidated. I think even then I saw that the single life, the celibate life, was to be part of God's plan, and I didn't rebel against it. *I think all along the line I felt a great sense of privilege at being able to share the Gospel, and that God had chosen, and was going to use me.* That might sound naive to some people, but to me it was like a flowering of my life. The beauty of the flower was for God[2] (emphasis mine).

How different the world would be without the contribution of Eva Burrows!

Some single adults just never think of themselves as "single adults." Dr. Evelyn Ramsey (1929–1989) was a medical missionary in Swaziland and New Guinea and a skilled linguist. Her work prompted a week-long coverage by NBC's "Today Show."[3]

Dr. Ramsey explained, "I am a person, important enough for Jesus Christ, God's Son, to die for me. When He did, He also chose me for a special calling and then helped me fulfill that calling one step at a time."

Evelyn Ramsey attended Tufts University Medical School during a time when few women sought careers in medicine. She survived financially by eating horsemeat sandwiches and using scraps of soap left on the shower room floors.

"I have not been swamped with romantic appeals, but I must be honest and say that I have done a little daydreaming that just the right person might appear on the horizon. I have also had some very impractical offers along this line which I clearly knew to be outside God's will for my life."

Her sense of discipline and commitment kept her from saying "yes" just to be married. Why didn't she marry?

"Sometimes I've felt like an express freight train zooming through a small town. I had no intention of stopping regardless of what I passed. My life was always 'full speed ahead' toward something bigger and better . . . I have never wanted anything to conflict with the contract I made with God when He called me to work for Him."

Can you say that: I have never wanted anything to conflict with my commitment to God? Years later, Evelyn looked back over her life and reassessed some of the choices she had made.

"Perhaps, I've given too wide a berth to various friendships, thinking they would result in an entanglement which would prevent me from keeping my part of the contract . . . I have always had a sense of a meter running and not having enough time if I didn't keep going. I have always felt I did not want to miss what God had in mind for me to do for Him."[3]

This talented woman who spent her forties practicing medicine in Africa, nearing retirement, looked back and concluded:

> There would not have been any way I could have
> Read the books I have read
> Written the words I have written
> Gone to the places I have gone
> Studied the courses I have studied
> Learned the languages I have learned
> Maintained the schedule I have maintained
> Mended the people I have mended
> If I had been encumbered by a husband and family.[4]

Henrietta Mears worked thirty-four years as Christian education director of the First Presbyterian Church of Hollywood, California. It seemed the whole continent was her parish. Over 400 of her single adults went into full-time Christian ministry. She was enormously effective as a single adult. She often said, "I just want to witness to the fact that wherever the Lord puts you, if He puts you on an island of the sea some place with Himself, He absolutely satisfies you."[5]

Henrietta's positive singleness as a role model led many young single women in her church to declare, "Oh, Miss Mears, I want to be just like you." Henrietta Mears didn't consider such statements as compliments.

"Nonsense," she retorted. "The Lord intends for you to marry. . . . " But, she admitted, "It has pleased me to know that they have been able to see my happiness and my complete satisfaction in the life that the Lord has given me."[6]

Not all fortysomethings have been as positive a model as Eva Burrows, Evelyn Ramsey, or Henrietta Mears.

PERSPECTIVES

I am a devotee of professional wrestling. I know that much of the action is faked but I am fascinated with the ability of the wrestlers and promoters to make the crowd—either in the arena or in the television audience—think it is real. I am particularly taken with tag team wrestling. There are two men in the ring. Each has a partner outside the ropes waiting to be tagged in. When the partner inside the ring has had it, he claws or crawls his way to the corner and extends his hand. His partner touches his fingertips and the fresh partner comes in if the referee sees the tag.

Tag team wrestling is much like mid-life and singleness—a partnership. The two phenomena compound one another.

A lot of people have difficulty being forty, married or single. And a lot of people have difficulty being single regardless of their age. But combine the two and you have a more complex opponent. Some people are fighting a two-front war (and the issue becomes even more complex if you are a single parent with teenagers who are trying to find themselves).

Let's consider four perspectives as we face the formidable tag team, "Forty and Single!"

Forty and Single: A Problem. For some, being forty and unmarried is a significant problem. Particularly for those who had not expected to be single, at least, not at age forty. Whether we have never married or have found ourselves single, via divorce or the death of a mate, many of us are beset by occasional bouts of the "poor mes."

The temptation for us is that the longer we are single, the bigger the problem becomes. If you see your status as a problem, you need to honestly ask: Would my mid-life transition be all that different if I were married? Certainly, the physiological realities would still be in place. Moreover, the complicated tensions of living with another person would merely alter the emotional landscape.

Forty and Single: A Tragedy. Some people see singleness as a tragedy. I have heard married people talk about how "good a wife and mother" a single adult would have been *if only* she had married. These people regard singles like choice apples left on the tree or grapes on the vine—hanging helplessly. This is a sad attitude.

Single adults who have been exposed to such thinking often

indict themselves: "It's all my fault!" Some subject themselves to intensely brutal put-downs: "Who would want to go out with me?" Others, however, usually have no idea why they have not found someone or been found.

Profile of a Fortysomething: Catherine Beecher (1800–1878). Pioneer educator and advocate of limited women's rights. Catherine's fiancé, Alexander Fish, drowned in a shipwreck. In Catherine's day, after such tragedies, it was considered a thing of honor for the fiancée never to marry.

Due to the male mortality rate, there were thousands of such women, forced by society's norm to live meaningless lives (remember they could not work in public). Some were left destitute or subject to the whims of married siblings. In the South, after the death of parents, many "old maids" lived with married brothers or sisters and became glorified "help" around the house in exchange for room and board (although this often led to conflict with their sisters-in-law). Catherine Clinton writing of women in the plantation South observed, "The spinster represented a potential source of labor that the family circle could, without hesitation, exploit for 'the family's sake.' "[7] There was no point in protesting since there were no economic alternatives.

However, Catherine Beecher decided to do something about her "tragedy." In 1823 she emerged from a severe depression and committed her life to education. She founded the Hartford Female Seminary, one of the nations' first schools for women; previously, women were tutored at home, subject to the dictates of the father. In 1832, she moved to what was then frontier, Cincinnati, and founded the Western Female Institute, training women to be teachers. In those days, there was no "sphere of usefulness" for an unmarried woman, but Miss Beecher believed that teaching school offered a great opportunity for women to use their minds and make a positive contribution to the public good.

Catherine had to convince men that females could be disciplinarians. She insisted, "Our Creator designed women to be the chief educators of our race and the prime minister of our family state, and our aim is to train her for this holy calling and to give her every possible advantage for the performance of its many and difficult duties."[8]

Catherine trained a generation of school marms who helped tame the West. She also introduced such innovations as calisthenics, guidance counseling, and what eventually became home economics in public education.

Compare Catherine's positive response to tragedy, to that demonstrated by Joseph Alston, elected Governor of South Carolina in 1812. As Aaron Burr's son-in-law, he was wealthy and had a tremendous future. However, just before his election, his son died. Then, in January, a month after his election, his wife of eleven years, Theodosia, died at sea enroute to visit her father. Governor Alston, thirty-one years old at the time (that day's equivalent of mid-life), was devastated.

His father-in-law tried to enlist him as a supporter of Andrew Jackson, thinking that would stir him out of his depression. Two days after Valentine's Day, the grieving governor wrote that while he agreed in sentiment, "the spirit, the energy, the health necessary to give such practical effect to sentiment, are all gone. *I feel too much alone, too entirely unconnected with the world, to take much interest in anything.*"[9] Today, too many fortysomethings could say the same thing.

After his lackluster service as governor, Alston retired from politics and died four years later. It was indeed a tragedy.

Forty and Single: A Transition. "And they lived happily ever after" is a common ending for fairy tales. Many people expect the same for their lives: Once they are married it's "home free." Then, by death or divorce they find themselves residents in "Singleland" again.

Some know they want to marry again. Indeed, Americans

are a remarrying people. Two-thirds of those who are divorced will remarry, many within eighteen months. Statistically, men remarry more quickly than do women.[10]

Increasingly, if the mother has custody of the children, she remains single longer, perhaps permanently.

I have created a few stirs in my seminars by sharing my conviction that a person should wait two to four years after a divorce to remarry. Many of my colleagues in single adult ministry share the same belief. The longer the time for healing, the better the chance for a successful second marriage.

It is important to embrace this single-again season and to learn its lessons. Allow time for the scabs to become scars before entering into another serious relationship. Time puts issues into perspective and heals thoroughly.

Forty and Single: An Opportunity. In my seminars, I insist that individuals will either see their singleness as a problem or as an opportunity. I consider myself a salesman for the "opportunities" of singleness.

George Rogers Clark comes to mind. As a young Virginia militiaman he had quite a reputation as a military leader and as a ladies' man. After the American Revolution, the Americans had an incredible appetite for the western frontier lands (now Ohio, Indiana, Illinois, and Michigan) which were still firmly in British hands. Clark realized that as long as the British held the Northwest, the western expansion could never be accomplished. This persuasive bachelor convinced the Virginia legislature to support the Kentucky frontiersmen with militia, supplies, and money.

Clark, by the sheer force of his personality, vision, and will, developed small bands of men into an incredible guerrilla force. He defeated the British and won their surrender on February 25, 1779 and opened the land for settlement.

However, he received no pay for his services during the engagement. Moreover, the Virginia legislature refused to even reimburse the general for his expenses, such as gunpowder, food, and supplies essential to the victory.

As a result, he lost a great deal of his own estate. Clark had to say "no" to marriage to Terese de Leyba—sister of the

French military commander of St Louis—because he no longer had the means to support her in the style to which she was accustomed. Two hearts were broken.

Clark gained the Northwest Territory for the new United States of America but lost almost everything he owned to do so. His sense of opportunity was only recognized by a grateful nation in Clark's old age.[11]

An Old Testament story speaks to this issue of opportunity. Ordinarily, women could not inherit property in ancient times, or for that matter in early American history. Land and valuables were inherited by males. In Jewish history, when it came time to divide up the land the Israelites had conquered, five courageous unmarried women, daughters of Zelophehad, of the tribe of Manasseh, realized that they had been "left out."

Rather than sit around saying "poor us" they decided to do something. They challenged the tradition: "Well, nothing personal, that's just the way we've always done it."

Mahlah, Noah, Hoglah, Milcah, and Tirzah appeared at the Tent of Meeting and requested the help of Moses. They needed an exception to tradition. Notice their strategy.

(1) *These single women had a genuine grievance.* Because their father had no male heirs, if the tradition was followed, then, their father's inheritance disappeared. So, boldly they asked for the inheritance. That must have sent the traditionalists fuming.

"Why should our father's name disappear from his clan, [they argued] because he had no son? Give us property among our father's relatives" (Num. 27:4). Property would give these single women standing in the community of Israel.

(2) *These single women came with a humble attitude.* They did not demand their rights because under Jewish law and tradition they had no rights. But by appealing to their father's name, they perhaps reminded other fathers who had no son(s) of the precariousness of their riches.

(3) *These single women came in the context of their faith.* They must have been unusual women to have had such courage to approach Moses. They came strengthened by their faith.

(4) *These single women's desire was noble.* In a time period with
no social security, no welfare, no employment opportunities
for young unmarried women, with status somewhat blemished
(they had no father to negotiate with a potential groom), who
would look after them? Why should they become burdens to
others? Give us, they suggested, what belonged to our fathers
and what would have been ours if we had been born male.

Moses "brought their case before the Lord" (Num. 27:5).
He recognized the precariousness of the women's status, but
he also realized he wanted the direction of the Lord. Moses,
as well as the women, realized the implications could be far
reaching.

I am awed by realizing that God Almighty became personally involved with the future of five single women.

"What Zelophehad's daughters are saying is right," [God
told Moses. Can you see Moses' brow shoot up: "It is?"].
"You must certainly give them property as an inheritance
among their father's relatives and turn their father's inheritance over to them" (Num. 27:7).

Here is a wonderful precedent: God declares that what
these women had said was correct. He didn't suggest that
Moses grant their request. He ordered, using the word "certainly." Moreover, it was not an "out-of-court" settlement or
"half a pie is better than none." God ordered that the whole
inheritance was to go to these single women. Whoever stood
to gain the inheritance under the old system must have been
disappointed by God's generosity.

(5) *The courage of these women produced long-term results.* Today, in courts, attorneys often urge judges' decisions to set a
precedent. When the law is not clear, a judge's reasoning can
be accepted by other judges in other courts.

God also said to Moses, "If a man dies and leaves no son,
turn his inheritance over to his daughter" (Num. 27:8).

As a result of these women's petition, an ad hoc solution
became part of the permanent legal code for Israel.[12]

Sometime later, the elders of the tribe of Manasseh came
back for clarification, asking what would happen if these wom-
en married outside their tribe. In essence, they were con-

cerned that portions of Zelophehad's inheritance could be lost.

Again, Moses consulted God. And again God gave direction. "They may marry anyone they please as long as they marry within the tribal clan of their father" (Num. 36:6). Again, precedent was set when God said, "Every daughter who inherits land in any Israelite tribe must marry someone in her father's tribal clan" (Num. 36:8).

Was there a fairy tale ending? Perhaps. But Scripture adds, "So Zelophehad's daughters did as the Lord commanded Moses" (Num. 36:10). What a testimony. What if that could be said of more fortysomethings today?

From this passage, I conclude that single adults who are fortysomething are not to put their lives on hold—waiting, whining, whimpering.

Instead, we are to do something. Zelophehad's daughters remind fortysomethings:

- to air genuine grievances to keep our attitudes humble;
- to deal with issues in the context of our faith;
- to commit ourselves to noble desires, issues, and causes;
- and to realize that our lives and decisions can have long-term impacts.

CONCLUSION

Zelophehad's unmarried daughters were not angry firebrands, rebels, or bra-burners. They were not defiant, caustic, or arrogant. They were simply women who believed that they were injured and limited by tradition.

Four thousand years later, single adults can look back to these courageous single women and say "Thank you."

How did these women see their singleness: As a problem? Perhaps initially. As a tragedy? Perhaps initially. But it is far more likely they perceived this season as an opportunity.

This Bible story clearly raises a question for single adults. What should we be doing today to deal with the injustices and inequities within our society, our economy, and our churches that limit or restrict the potential of single adults?

QUESTIONS

1. How can mid-life be turned into a growth experience?
2. What is your worth as a human being based on?
3. Who are you at this point in your life?
4. Have you allowed romance to conflict with your commitment to God?
5. In what ways do you see this season? As an opportunity? A tragedy? A transition?

Chapter Four

KEEP IN THE MIDDLE
OF THE ROAD

*Truly life begins at forty or thereabout. Mid-
life is the time when we weigh our wishes on
the scale of reality. Our picture-wishes,
drawn and detailed over a long period of
years, need fresh color, revised lines, and new
shapes. Yet, how painful . . .*
— *Peter L. Steinke*

**GOAL FOR FORTYSOMETHINGS: To mature
spiritually.**

Mary Bethune, founder of Bethune-Cookman College relied
on the generosity of wealthy northern capitalists who wintered
in Daytona Beach, to support her college. She organized
groups of singers who would sing black spirituals outside the
hotels. One of Mrs. Bethune's favorites was "Keep In the
Middle of the Road." One line of the song says "Don't turn to
the right, don't turn to the left, but keep in the middle of the
road." Fortysomething is a time to keep in the middle of the
road spiritually.[1]

The season of fortysomething is a time to reexamine the
spiritual issues of life. In fact, scholars suggest that "religious
spiritual interests may increase" during this time of crisis and
transition. J. Bill Ratliff says that we end up asking questions
like:

- Where is God in all the changes of my life?
- Is there any order to events?
- Where do I fit in the scheme of things?
- What is the meaning of change?
- What is God's call to me, at this time in my life?[2]

John Nesbitt, a specialist on change explained, "When people are buffeted about by change, the need for spiritual belief intensifies. Most seek reassurance in one of two ways: either through inner-directed 'trust the feeling inside' movements or through outer-directed 'this is the way it is' authoritarian religions. Both are flourishing today."[3]

Indeed, this may account for the growing contention of many researchers that baby boomers are rediscovering the church. Today American religion offers a smorgasbord—Eastern religions, New Age, fundamentalism, mainline denominations. Simply, a deep religious vacuum exists in contemporary civilization and an abundance of zealous vendors are offering solutions. Fortysomethings are looking for something to satisfy their spiritual hunger. Many fortysomethings who ignored or abandoned organized religion a decade or so ago, "are returning to church with their children in tow or joining the New Age movement."[4]

Billy Graham in a powerful essay on faith in "The Courage of Conviction," identified these questions as vital to spiritual and emotional meaning:

(1) Who am I?
(2) Why am I here?
(3) Where did I come from and where am I going?
(4) Does God exist, and if so, does it make any difference?
(5) Can I know God?[5]

What are fortysomethings to believe? To stake their lives on? Andrew Greeley, Catholic priest and sociologist said, "Either there is a plan and purpose—and that plan and purpose can best be described by the words life and love—or we live in a cruel, arbitrary, and deceptive cosmos in which our lives are a brief transition between two oblivions."[6]

In the midst of mid-life, when psychological tempests rage, many fortysomethings find the courage to reexamine their spiritual moorings and commitments. Sadly, some discover that they have grown up in the church without knowing Jesus. Others discover that they have grown up without being rooted in Scripture or in sound doctrine.

George Gallup, Jr. has thoroughly researched the current American fascination with religious faith and observed, "While religion has powerful appeal for Americans . . . surveys indicate that even if religion is an important force in our lives *it is not the center of our lives*. It does not have primacy. Interest may be high, but commitment is often low"[7] (emphasis mine).

Let's ask ourselves these questions: Is faith an important part of my life? Can my faith weather this mid-life crisis or transition? If not, how do I develop such a mature faith?

For many fortysomethings, Chuck Colson contends, "Faith is but a notation on their resumes and [their] ornate churches are but a reflection of their social status."[8]

WHAT DO I REALLY BELIEVE?

Mid-life is a time when many fortysomethings hit the spiritual "wall." A faith that has been mature enough to meet life's challenges and opportunities, may now seem inadequate to handle the issues directly in one's path. Peter Benson, president of Research Institute, defines "faith maturity" as "integrating a deep personal relationship with a loving God, and an active commitment to serving others."[9]

Many fortysomethings wonder how they can help others when so many issues appear in a spiritual fog. Moreover, in some congregations, silence on the issue of mid-life suggests that the church doesn't take the transition seriously. Some pastors offer advice that is the equivalent of, "Take two aspirin and you'll feel better in the morning."

For those individuals who are alone, struggling through mid-life, "What do I believe?" becomes a very pertinent question. Simply, one's response to mid-life is shaped largely by one's faith.

TIME FOR RENEWAL

In my own case, turning forty was a time for spiritual renewal. I needed an adult faith that matched the realities of my life.

Renewal was stimulated by reading Philip Watson's *Let God Be God* about Martin Luther. Martin Luther understood the Scriptural injunction against "bowing down to graven images" included mental images since "false doctrine is no less an idol than a heathen stock or stone."[10] Moreover, Martin Luther concluded, "We must examine ourselves in the light of God's commandments, to see how the Spirit's work progresses, and how much yet remains to be done, lest we grow careless and we think we have already reached the goal."[11]

How is the work progressing?

In June 1987, while writing about Corrie ten Boom, I learned of her love of J.B. Phillips' New Testament translation and began reading my copy. First John 1 "exploded" in my heart.

If we refuse to admit that we are sinners, then we live in a world of illusion and truth becomes a stranger to us. But if we freely admit that we have sinned, we find Him reliable and just — He forgives our sins and makes us thoroughly clean from all that is evil. For if we say "we have not sinned," we are making Him a liar and cut ourselves off from what He has to say to us (1 John 1:8-10, PH).

As I read devotionally 1 John in the Phillips, I became more convicted of my need for renewal. After all, "we have one who speaks to the Father in our defense — Jesus Christ, the Righteous One" (1 John 2:1).

I have found a liberating freedom in freely admitting my sin. I have found a Saviour who can handle sin. I have found, at fortysomething, God to be as "reliable and just" as John promised.

Moreover, I, like thousands of others, have a hunger for renewal through ritual. At mid-life I want more ritual and less toe-tapping. I want more corporate confession of sin. I want more fellowship around the communion table and the altar.

And I want an atmosphere in worship that is distinctively different than a pep rally. I want to kneel in the presence of a holy and sovereign God.

Fortunately for my spiritual hunger, we are in the midst of a renaissance of ritualism that is slowly spreading across a wide spectrum of religious traditions. I am not alone. Other fortysomethings hunger for faith expressions that have historical as well as theological meaning.

Indeed, too many fortysomethings lug heavy emotional and spiritual issues into Sunday morning services only to find the "chatty informalism" and "entertainment Christianity" as expressed through smoozing and religious monologues and a parade of high professionalism on the platform, isn't easing the burden. We are being starved by worship services that are so I-me-my centered that the sovereignty of God is lost. At the other end of the theological spectrum are pastors who are always telling individuals to "shape up" but never *how* to do it.

Indeed, the struggle for renewal, for a fortysomething faith, may put us at odds with friends, family, who take great comfort in singing, "It was good for our fathers, it was good for our mothers . . . then it's good enough for me."

The old time religion won't cut it in the nineties for many fortysomethings. We need a faith that makes a difference in the way we think and live and the way we spend our money. We need a faith that is more than a religious extension of Americanism. We need a faith that is more than cutesy little choruses in the key of C. We need to hear from courageous prophets that one can not have it "all" and have Jesus too.

We need to hear that grace is costly. Many fortysomethings long for a radical faith that makes a difference. Many fortysomethings will settle for what a single adult martyr, Dietrich Bonhoeffer, called "cheap grace." "Cheap grace is grace without discipleship, grace without the Cross, grace without Jesus Christ."[12] "Grace is costly," Bonhoeffer argued, "because it costs a man his life, and it is grace because it gives a man the only true life. It is costly because it condemns sin, and grace because it justifies the sinner."[13]

I have found great nourishment in *The Book of Common Prayer* (1789) used in the Episcopal Church. When a congregation witnesses the baptism of new Christians, the celebrant or minister invites the congregation, "Let us join with those who are committing themselves to Christ and *renew* our own baptismal covenant."[14] From time to time we need to take stock—to take a spiritual inventory—in order to renew our commitments.

I have found that the questions asked of candidates for baptism in the Episcopal Church, are very appropriate for fortysomethings to ask. Let's take time and review the basics that determine what we believe.

FAITH QUESTIONS FOR FORTYSOMETHINGS
Question 1: Do you believe in God the Father? Do you believe in Jesus Christ, the Son of God? Do you believe in God the Holy Spirit?[15]

Maybe we should insert a *"still"* between you and believe in these questions. By mid-life, some of us are not as sure of what we believe as we once were.

The Apostle's Creed answers the questions orthodoxly. The creed is an ancient but richly contemporary declaration worthy of our respect but to some fortysomethings, it's just meaningless words. Read it aloud:

I believe in God the Father Almighty, Maker of heaven and earth:

And in Jesus Christ His only Son, our Lord; who was conceived by the Holy Spirit, born of the Virgin Mary, suffered under Pontius Pilate, was crucified, dead, and buried; He descended into hell; the third day He rose again from the dead; He ascended into heaven, and sitteth on the right hand of God, the Father Almighty; from thence He shall come to judge the living and the dead.

I believe in the Holy Spirit, the holy catholic church, the communion of saints, the forgiveness of sins, the resurrection of the body, and the life everlasting. Amen.

The contemporary Apostle's Creed is a direct descendant of the *Rituale Romanum*, or Old Roman Creed first recited around A.D. 150 and developed as a protection for candidates from the heresies of the early church's detractors. Much of today's text was added through the *Textus Receptus* in the eighth century.

Theologian William M. Greathouse noted, "The creed is the faith of the church and not of the individual as such. *Credo* ("I believe") is the believer's personal signature to the apostolic witness."[16]

DO YOU BELIEVE IN GOD THE FATHER?
In your experience, who is God today? Philip Watson wrote that in Luther's experience there was only one question: the question of God. Many of us could be indicted by J.B. Phillips' title: *Your God Is Too Small.*[17]

I have had difficulty in trusting God. I've found it hard to accept His fatherhood, because I was emotionally estranged from my own father for many years. I saw God like my earthly father—someone that I could not please and who was emotionally distant. I read the Word of God but I could not fall in love with God.

My renewal began with a passage from 2 Samuel, "God does not take away life; instead, He devises ways so that a banished person may not remain estranged from Him" (14:14). These words support Jonah's confession, "You are a gracious and compassionate God, slow to anger and abounding in love" (Jonah 4:2).

I am finding at age forty-three that I can now appreciate God as the Father described in Psalm 103 better than I could at twelve, twenty-two, or thirty-two.

The Lord is compassionate and gracious,
    slow to anger, abounding in love.
He will not always accuse,
    nor will He harbor His anger forever;
He does not treat us as our sins deserve
    or repay us according to our iniquities.

For as high as the heavens are above the earth,
  so great is His love for those who fear Him;
as far as the east is from the west,
  so far has He removed our transgressions from us.
As a father has compassion on his children,
  so the Lord has compassion on those who fear Him;
for He knows how we are formed,
He remembers that we are dust (Ps. 103:8-14).

This is the God I am trusting—a God almost too good to be true. In these times, you need to know who you believe in. I have been influenced by Bruce Larson who wrote:

God's love does not depend on any virtue in us or on our achievement. . . . But the nature of His love is such that He does not leave us as He finds us. When someone begins the adventure of faith, God says to him, in effect: "I am going to begin to change you. Programmed into your inner computer, through glands and genes and circumstances and experiences, is an inability to love totally. I love you so much that I want to change all of those intricate wires of experience, sense, and thought that make you an unknowable, unrelatable person. It may take a thousand years of reprogramming to make you a lover of people, or Me, and of yourself, but I promise that I will continue relentlessly until you have been totally transformed. . . . I'll not stop until all your quirks and defense mechanisms and subterfuges and alibis are gone and you are a transparent, relatable person . . . I am not trying to change you so that I can love you. I love you, and because I do, I want to change you."[18]

Profile of a Fortysomething: William Cowper
(1731–1800). English hymnwriter. Although born into a minister's home, he was devastated as a boy by his mother's death and by the constant bullying he received in school. Eventually, William Cowper graduated with a law

degree but in the process had an emotional breakdown and even attempted suicide. From 1763 to 1765 he was institutionalized. Despite brilliance and promise, William Cowper could not handle life.

During one bout of depression, he ordered his driver to a nearby river, where he intended to take his own life. Somehow the driver became lost and finally Cowper's mood lifted and they returned home.

Some have linked this experience with his great hymn, "God Moves in A Mysterious Way." However, the suicide attempt occurred *after* he wrote the hymn in June, 1773, at age forty-two.

William Cowper's hymn offers insight into God:

God moves in a mysterious way
His wonders to perform;
He plants His footsteps in the sea
And rides upon the storm.
You fearful saints, fresh courage take;
The clouds you so much dread
Are big with mercy, and shall break
In blessing on your head.
Judge not the Lord by feeble sense
But trust Him for His grace;
Behind a frowning providence
Faith sees a smiling face.

Cowper also composed, "There Is a Fountain Filled With Blood" a remarkably clear hymn of grace, became a confidant of John Newton, who wrote, "Amazing Grace," and helped edit a popular hymnbook, *Olney Hymns.*

This bachelor had known love. He had fallen in love with his cousin, but family opposition—based on his unstable mental history—blocked their marriage. They parted and never saw each other again; neither married.[19]

God uses those who are available to Him. Cowper's profile proves that even severely depressed people can make a lasting contribution.

DO YOU BELIEVE IN JESUS CHRIST, THE SON OF GOD?

The name of Jesus is on the lips of a lot of people but what does He mean to you—in the middle of your forties wilderness? Jesus never went through a mid-life crisis, but He did sweat blood. And He did suffer when He was tempted. And He was betrayed and crucified.

Many Christians have been so anxious to defend Christ's deity, that they have been oblivious to His humanity. Jesus "had to be made like His brothers *in every way*" the writer of Hebrews declared (Heb. 2:17, emphasis mine). He had to firsthand understand temptation, in order to be able to "help those who are being tempted" (Heb. 2:18). Moreover, "we do not have a high priest who is unable to sympathize with our weaknesses, but we have one who has been tempted in every way, just as we are—yet was without sin" (Heb. 4:15).

We permit Jesus to be human only from the waist up. We have ignored the testimony of His circumcision, thinking that was only a detail to demonstrate His Jewishness rather than His maleness. We have conveniently—because of our discomfort—overlooked Paul's declaration: "Being made in human likeness. And being found in appearance as a man" (Phil. 2:7-8).

Do you think Jesus was only tempted to jump off the pinnacle of the temple? To turn stones into bread? To worship Satan? I think those were only appetizers on the temptation menu that Jesus faced.

The Good News is held out to fortysomethings by the author of Hebrews, "Let us then approach the throne of grace with confidence, so that we may receive mercy and find grace to help us in our time of need" (Heb. 4:16).

Few men have left a more lasting testimony on grace than Judge Robert E. B. Baylor, who at forty-eight years of age became judge of the Third District of Texas—before Texas was admitted to the Union. Baylor had served in both the Kentucky and Alabama legislatures; he represented Alabama in Congress from 1829 to 1831, but was defeated for reelection. Baylor had never married, no doubt due to seeing his fianée thrown from her horse and dragged to death. The Republic of Texas offered this single adult a fresh start. As a prominent jurist and member of the Supreme Court, Baylor who was a Baptist minister, rode from town to town, following a predictable pattern: he preached grace on Sunday and administered justice on Monday. Often at night Baylor conducted religious services. Defendants came to Baylor's meetings hoping to influence the judge's mercy the following day in court. Baylor believed in the great grace of God. He noted, "I should have preferred to have passed away to the land hereafter in silence, for such a poor sinner as I am deserves not to have any notice taken of him."[20]

Baylor depreciated his own sermons which he described as "very feeble." "I had many difficulties including my ignorance of the Scriptures." However, "a sense of the mercy of God toward such a sinner as I, would overwhelm me [How many fortysomethings can identify with that statement?] and frequently in prayer and attempting to preach I would burst into tears . . . I pity the man who cannot shed a tear over his own sins and those of his fellow mortals. Jesus wept that we might weep."[21]

This single adult practitioner of grace helped start the first Baptist educational society in Texas and helped found and endow Baylor University.

DO YOU BELIEVE IN THE HOLY SPIRIT?

Jesus, as a single adult, had a close relationship with the disciples, particularly John, and with single adults like Lazarus, Mary, and Martha. Jesus comforted His followers by saying, "And I will ask the Father, and He will give you another Counselor to be with you forever—the Spirit of Truth. I will not leave you as orphans" (John 14:16, 18). That promise is still in effect.

In the Greek the word is *paraclete*, the Helper or the One who comes alongside. What does this Holy Spirit do?

- Mediates to men and women the glorified Christ
- Continues Christ's work in the world

- Creates and vitalizes the church
- Administers salvation
- Intercedes for men and women
- Inspires, preserves, and illuminates Scripture

Arnold Airhart, a Canadian theologian, says the Holy Spirit is "God-close-at-hand," universally present. Moreover, "the Spirit makes Christianity morally pungent, personally real, and gives it life-changing power."[22]

Paul said, "The Spirit Himself testifies with our spirit that we are God's children" (Rom. 8:16) especially when our hearts condemn us (1 John 3:20). Paul declared "that your body is a temple of the Holy Spirit" (1 Cor. 6:19).

The Holy Spirit wants to be a comforter during this time of crisis or transition called fortysomething. Will you let Him?

CONCLUSION

Few men have preached more effectively in America than a single adult named Francis Asbury, the first Bishop of the Methodist Church in America. Francis Asbury never married and gave his life to his scattered congregations.

More than 20,000 people turned out for his funeral in Baltimore in 1816. The text for the funeral sermon is an appropriate one for fortysomethings today to seriously consider: "But thou hast fully known my doctrine, manner of life, purpose, faith, longsuffering, charity, patience" (2 Tim. 3:10, KJV).[23]

Who knows your doctrine, the piers of your faith? It is more than knowing facts about God, Jesus, and the Holy Spirit. *It is knowing God that counts.*

In the next chapter, we will examine how these doctrinal commitments to God the Father, God the Son, and God the Holy Spirit influence every arena of our lives.

QUESTIONS

1. How have you been aware of God's presence in your life during this time of transition?
2. Is God the center of your life or merely an important force in your life? What commitments would you have to make

to let God be more relevant in your life?

3. What specific spiritual disciplines do you regularly practice: prayer, meditation, fasting, journaling? As a result of reading *Fortysomething and Single* can you identify one to begin practicing?

4. Have you settled for what Bonhoeffer called "a cheap grace"?

5. Do you feel comfortable thinking about Jesus as human and as male? What makes you uncomfortable?

6. After reading this chapter, what is God saying to you?

Chapter Five

SHAPING A FORTYSOMETHING FAITH

Well, who wants to be young anyhow? Any idiot born in the last forty years can be young, and besides forty-five isn't really old, it's right on the border.

— *Ogden Nash*

GOAL FOR FORTYSOMETHINGS: To develop a deep personal relationship with a loving God.

In the last chapter, we reexamined our beliefs about God, Jesus, and the Holy Spirit. Many fortysomethings essentially crave the same thing: a tie between their everyday lives and the transcendent. One commentator noted, "The way religion is presented traditionally has spoken to our inner selves less and less. People want a living, feeling experience of spirituality. They want to get in touch with the soul."[1]

In a culture such as ours, experiencing rapid social change and crisis, we need a faith that is relevant—an unapologetic commitment. We need to know why we have believed what we do.

Some Christians would argue that doctrine is boring, dull, and incomprehensible for the average person. Others have simply concluded, I may not know the what of faith but I do know the who. To offset these let's continue our questions from *The Book of Common Prayer.*

Question 2: Will you continue in the apostles' teaching and fellowship, in the breaking of bread, and in the prayers?

They key word is *continue* to keep ourselves in a fellowship of believers. We live in a do-it-yourself age with books and tapes on how to solve any problem from repairing cars to curing ourselves of cancer. James Davidson Hunter contends that most evangelicals are caught in what he terms "the quandary of modernity," at least mildly embarrassed by socially unacceptable doctrines, like hell. Some zealous singles boast, "I don't drink, dance, or chew, or go with girls who do!"

But a lot of us "want to." Many fortysomethings have a nagging sense of not belonging to the *real* world. We're afraid that we may be uninvited to the real party. We may be left out.

Dr. Hunter notes that historically the church relied on the wisdom of older saints, prayer, and fasting when it confronted stress with its culture or when believers wrestled with personal issues. We, instead, have turned to a "functional rationalism" or "religious pragmatism," so that through seminars, cassettes, and teachings that present prepackaged techniques we attempt to resolve our spiritual "jams" and dilemmas. "We have a certainty that all our problems can be solved *if* we can just find the right techniques."[2]

I know that I have a sense of confidence about the resources that I have at my disposal. And that it is very rare for me to confess to God, "I don't have the resources to take care of _____ ." But I am learning that He wants me to rely on Him.

It's hard to wait on the Lord. It's easy to implement spiritual disciplines *my* way on *my* schedule. I can do it right after work, and just before racquetball. The one minute Christian: self-sufficient and efficient — how convenient!

No wonder I am convicted by the following: "Now Thomas (called Didymus), [the doubter] one of the Twelve, was *not with the disciples* when Jesus came" (John 20:24). Have you ever missed an awesome spiritual moment because you were play-

ing spiritual Lone Ranger? Today, the verse could be true of a
lot of fortysomethings: "Now, Harold, one of the group members, was not with the believers when Jesus came." How sad.
We need others for our spiritual growth. Bill Hybels says that
significant spiritual relationships "aren't luxuries for believers.
They're absolute necessities" for survival.[3] We need each
other.

*Question 3: Will you persevere in resisting evil, and, when-
ever you fall into sin, repent and return to the Lord?*

I have often taught on David's sexual affair with Bathsheba,
as detailed in 2 Samuel 11. Some who have preached that text
have begun with the faulty assumption that it was all
Bathsheba's fault. If she had been inside taking a bath in the
first place, none of it would ever have happened!

Then why didn't the text begin with the bathtub rather
than, "In the spring, at the time when kings go off to
war . . . *David remained in Jerusalem* (2 Sam. 11:1, emphasis
mine). Clearly, if David had been where he should have been,
in the field with his men, not in Jerusalem, no temptation
would have occurred.

David didn't repent until after Nathan confronted him. Until after the Lord came looking for him.

How can we persevere in resisting evil when the devil is
"like a roaring lion" (1 Peter 5:8). If the devil didn't leave
Jesus alone, should we expect to be ignored? The truth is,
Satan will harrass us. But our hope is this—when we are at our
weakest, exhausted from saying no we are only a breath from
victory.

For almost fifteen years I have carried a piece of paper in
my New Testament with sobering words written after a spiritual defeat:

> The tragedy of failure is to be able to see how close I was
> to success, that had I repeated our hope one more time the
> temptation might have passed and in passing made me
> stronger for the future.
>
> I came so close to success—and yet lost. And in losing, I
> found my weakness and confessed it.

The question is not whether we will fail—the wording of number three assumes we will. Rather, how long will we lie there? Will we hide like Adam and Eve? Professional football teams do not pay extravagant salaries to backs who drop the ball in the end zone and have temper tantrums. They pay enormous salaries to guys who get up, trot back to the huddle, and say, "Let me try it again." So it is with sin. Confess it now, and begin again this very moment.

Question 4· Will you proclaim by word and example the Good News of God in Christ?

Sometimes, non-Christians have a hard time believing in the God of some evangelicals. I have said to a few, "Tell me about your view of God. I might not believe in that God either."

Paul warned Timothy, "Don't let anyone look down on you because you are young [forty], but set an example for the believers [and nonbelievers] in speech, in life, in love, in faith, and in purity" (1 Tim. 4:12). Some fortysomethings wish Paul had quit with faith. Paul added, "Watch your life *and* doctrine closely (1 Tim. 4:15, emphasis mine). A lot of fortysomethings are straight as an arrow when it comes to orthodoxy. With the Rich Young Ruler they testify, "All these things have I kept" (Matt. 19:20).

But few people are attracted to Jesus through doctrine. They do want to know: Does faith work in your life? The Four Spiritual Laws have their place, but usually are not as effective as life-style witnessing.

Proclaiming the Gospel may mean being prepared for that golden moment of witnessing opportunity and taking care to see that our life does not contradict our doctrine.

Question 5: Will you seek and serve Christ in all persons, loving your neighbor as yourself?

In Jesus' day—as well as in ours—there were experts in the Law. People who have that ability to so phrase a question that it zings. Such an expert confronted Jesus.

"Teacher, . . . what must I do to inherit eternal life?"

[Many fortysomethings are asking the same thing.]

He answered, "Love the Lord your God with all your heart

and with all your soul and with all your strength and with all your mind." We often punctuate the verse by stopping here. Jesus, however, continued, "And, 'Love your neighbor as yourself' " (Luke 10:25-27).

The expert hedged—as do many fortysomethings—with a rhetorical question, "And who is my neighbor?" (Luke 10:29)

Jesus answered by telling the story of the Good Samaritan. The Good Samaritan found an injured man lying beside a roadway, bandaged his wounds, and "took him to an inn; and took care of him"—all of this because "he took pity on him" while the priest and the Levite ignored the man (Luke 10:33-34).

Jesus asked the questioner: Which of the three (priest/Levite/Samaritan) was "neighbor" to the man? The man replied, "The one who had mercy on him." Then Jesus admonished him, saying, "Go and do likewise" (Luke 10:37).

Profile of a Fortysomething: Elizabeth Cole (1911–   ). Nazarene missionary in Swaziland, Africa. As a young Montana teen, she broke broncos on a cattle ranch and rode herds with six brothers. During nurses' training in Billings she was converted and answered the call to become a missionary, even though she would have to give up her horses. Miss Cole was assigned to Africa in 1935. To her surprise, to reach outposts, she had to ride a horse. God had given her back her riding.

In 1937, the twenty-six-year-old Elizabeth learned that the British were organizing a new leprosy colony in Mbuluzi; Elizabeth sought permission to become a permanent resident of the colony. Her life was lonely. For stretches of weeks, the only visitor was a medical doctor. Yet, under Miss Cole's loving attention, the patients received excellent medical care.

One American visitor saw her cleaning the wounds of a leper and said, "I wouldn't do that for a million dollars!"

Miss Cole replied, "I wouldn't either . . . not for a million dollars, but I would for Christ."

> This fortysomething attracted the attention of Queen Elizabeth who honored her in 1960 for her outstanding service to British subjects. Miss Cole was the first American in Swaziland to receive this honor.[4]
>
> Where others saw lepers, Elizabeth Cole, a single adult, saw Christ.

In the days ahead, particularly with issues like the homeless, AIDS, and drugs, Christians will have to wrestle with our definitions of "neighbor." As fortysomethings we need to take time to get to know the people around us.

Question 6: Will you strive for justice and peace among all people, and respect the dignity of every human being?

Once we have recognized our neighbor, we are destined to do something about his or her needs. Today there is a growing fascination with a "what's in this for me?" faith. "Don't ask me to do something about the third world or the needy in my zip code!"

The mere mention of social justice or the social gospel brings a frown to many evangelicals. For the most part, we prefer a personal piety that can tolerate prejudices and rationalizations that help us sidestep all inconveniences. But we must remember the words of Martin Luther King who said, "Injustice anywhere is a threat to justice everywhere."[5]

Jesus said, "Whatever you did [do] for one of the least of these brothers of Mine, you did [do] for Me" (Matt. 25:40). It doesn't take a genius to figure out who "the least of these" is in today's world.

James prods fortysomethings, "Be doers of the Word, and not hearers only, deceiving yourselves" (James 1:22, NKJV). The proverbialist said, "To do what is right and just is more acceptable to the Lord than sacrifice" (Prov. 21:3), or prayer meetings or Bible studies I might add.

How do we ignore the prophets' words, "He has showed you, O man, what is good. And what does the LORD require of you? To act justly and to love mercy and to walk humbly with your God" (Micah 6:8). Three verbs—*act, love,* and *walk*—say it all. And let's face it—much of the Book of Acts does not square with the mood of middle-class American forty-somethings who have worked so hard to accumulate so much.

God expects us to be as involved as were the first-century Christians. Luke recorded, "All [not some] of the believers were one in heart and mind. No one claimed that any of his possessions was his own, but they shared everything they had. With great power the apostles continued to testify to the resurrection of the Lord Jesus, and much grace was with them all. *There were no needy persons among them*" (Acts 4:32-34, emphasis mine).

What an incredible accomplishment! No needy persons among them. Why? Because "from time to time those who owned lands or houses sold them, brought the money from the sales and put it at the apostles' feet, and it was distributed to anyone as he had need" (Acts 4:35).

Teach or preach that in the average single adult Sunday School class and get ready for an explosion. The reaction will demonstrate our "selective" or convenient attitude toward the interpretation of Scripture. Sadly, Tom Sine concluded, "In contemporary churches in which we expect little from our people, and are satisfied with even less, it is really hard for us to take Jesus' call to the Cross seriously."[6]

Vance Havner dealt with the issue straight-forwardly:

It is about time we stopped watering down our Lord's severe terms, His insistence on detachment in spirit if not in letter from all earthly concerns. We have reduced these to mere instances of glorified exaggeration, overstating a truth in order to drive it home. The result is a band of run-of-the-mill disciples who make little impact on this age because we are as they are. Our Lord lost many a prospect because He would not mark down the price of utter devotion. We fill our churches with these dime-a-dozen Christians who hear the Word and with joy receive it but crumble under persecution. We shall make poor progress until we can rally a persecuted minority, scorning the values of this world and living by stringent discipline.[7]

RENUNCIATIONS AND ADHERENCES

The next three questions we'll consider are called renunciations. To renounce is to give up, or resign, to refuse to follow, obey, or recognize any further.

Question 7: Do you renounce Satan and all the spiritual forces of wickedness that rebel against God?

Most of us are quick to renounce and denounce the devil. It's in vogue, these days to "bind Satan" and some can make quite a sensational display of it.

My friend Carl Hurley, a Kentucky humorist, tells a great tale on himself. He had dressed up as the devil for a Halloween party. He was walking to the party—in a stereotypical costume: red suit, pitchfork, horns—when a thunderstorm came up. Carl ran for shelter to a nearby church which happened to be having a prayer meeting.

When Carl came through the door the people began screaming and yelling and jumping out the windows to get away from him. One obese man got caught in the window; as Carl approached him, trying to calm him, the man announced, "I may have been a deacon for twenty-two years, but I've been on your side all along!"

Christians are adept at hunting secular humanists, pornographers and such, but we're not as good at finding secular materialists who snooze comfortably in our congregations; secular militarists who want to blow up half of the world or launch a major war in Latin America; polite racists, homophobics, sexists, or power-hungry controllers who want to run the church according to their personal agendas.

Question 8: Do you renounce the evil powers of this world which corrupt and destroy the creatures of God?

We're tough on hardcore pornographers who sell their wares in adult bookstores, but what about the softcore pornographers who use advertising to degrade women? What about the swimsuit issue of *Sports Illustrated?* What about the harmless practice of girl watching, which is no more than corporate lust?

Consider the growing antifemale attitudes among Christian males: that women should be taught a thing or two. Sexism smolders in the church and among many single adults. I've heard many angry, recently divorced men snarl, "All women are alike!" Sexism works both sides of the street. Some women lump all men into the category of their ex or men they have dated.

Evil blends into our lives too easily.

Question 9: Do you renounce all sinful desires that draw you from the love of God?

Robert Robinson wrote a hymn, "Come Thou Fount of Every Blessing," that gets to the very root of this question. The lyrics carry a potent message:

O to grace how great a debtor
Daily I'm constrained to be!
Let Thy goodness, like a fetter
Bind my wandering heart to Thee:
Prone to wander, Lord, I feel it,
Prone to leave the God I love.

"Prone to wander" describes the spiritual habits of many fortysomethings who have seasons of singing the spiritual equivalent of "I did it my way." We are easily drawn away from the love of God.

Frances Ridley Havergal, a never-married single adult who died at age forty-three, wrote the hymn, "Take My Life And Let It Be."

Take my life and let it be
Consecrated, Lord to Thee;
Take my hands and let them move
At the impulse of Thy love
At the impulse of Thy love.

Miss Havergal wrote verses that began

Take my *feet* and let them be . . .
Take my *lips* and let them be . . .
Take my *love*, my God I pour . . .

Some of us don't want to be led—especially at His pace. Miss Havergal certainly understood that. Through dark depressive spiritual times, she concluded, "I think that the great root of all my trouble and alienation is that I do not now make an unconditional surrender of myself to God: and until this is done I shall know no peace."[8]

There came a time when Frances prayed, "Oh that He would indeed purify me and make me white at any cost." She eventually concluded, before her death at forty-three, "God's crosses are often made of most unexpected and strange material."[9]

Crosses are often pitched between us and some of the greenest pastures in the world.

Many fortysomethings live with a gravitational tug to the values of this world. We hope the Lord won't approach our toy boxes, our comfort zones. Sometimes we want only a quarter's worth of Christianity, just enough to comfort us but not enough to complicate our lifestyles.

The last three questions we will study are called "adherences" or commitments. Most fortysomethings know what they were saved *from*, but few know what they were saved *to*.

Question 10: Do you turn to Jesus Christ and accept Him as your Saviour?

In the ancient tradition of the church, individuals were candidates for membership for years, so that their lives could be carefully watched for the signs of obedience and renunciation. They were awakened during the night before Easter dawn and led to the church. For hours they sat in darkness, facing the west.

Then at sunrise, they were physically turned to face the rising Easter sun. This symbolized the turning away from sin and turning toward the Light.

Today, after 2,000 years of experience, the church asks us to do the same thing as those early believers: to turn from sin and to turn toward the Light, Jesus. Turning is a decision, sometimes very painful, but those who have experienced the Light confirm it's always the right choice. As a fortysomething, have you *turned* to Jesus Christ?

Question 11: Do you put your whole trust in His grace and love?

Ephesians 2:8 couldn't be clearer, yet ironically there are those who prefer a Gospel of works or a combo: works *and* grace. "For it is by grace you have been saved, through faith — and this not from yourselves, it is the gift of God — not of works, so that no one can boast."

Protestants have always sung their theology. A fortysomething Christian educator, Julia Johnston, wrote:

Marvelous grace of our loving Lord
Grace that exceeds our sin and our guilt!
Yonder on Calvary's mount outpoured
There where the blood of the Lamb was spilt.
Marvelous, infinite, matchless grace,
Freely bestowed on all who believe.
You that are longing to see His face,
Will you this moment His grace receive?

What else can the chorus read than:

Grace, grace, God's grace
Grace that will pardon and cleanse within,
Grace, grace, God's grace
Grace that is greater than all our sin!

Admittedly, it can be risky putting one's *whole* trust on anyone. But Jesus never fails to guard our trust.

Question 12: Do you promise to follow and obey Him as your Lord?

We often sing in singles' gatherings the little chorus, "He Is Lord." Some like to personalize it and sing, "He's My Lord." Those words are easier to sing than to live, especially in the tough times when obedience is a burden.

CONCLUSION

We are in danger today of merely proclaiming an attractive Gospel. We offer religion that doesn't make you different but *better.* You're not called to give up anything, but simply to accept Jesus.

It's really too bad that those generations of saints that sang, "Take This Old World But Give Me Jesus" didn't have our enlightenment to know how to have it all: Jesus and the "all." Or would they have wanted our spiritual impoverishment which is a natural byproduct of such an attractive heresy?

This chapter closes with some tough words. In a pluralistic, technological society with little room for the holy, we need fortysomethings who know what they believe because they know in whom they have believed.

In the nineteenth century, a young Frenchman rode a train. At one stop, an old man boarded, sat down near the younger man and began to pray. The Frenchman became annoyed at the old man's piety.

"Old man," he interrupted, "do you still believe in that stuff? Don't you know that religion can't answer man's questions about the universe. Only science can!"

For the rest of the trip, the young man lectured the older passenger on the marvelous advances of science, the bright visions of the future. The old man kept praying.

When it was time for the young man to get off the train, he turned to his fellow passenger, and asked, "By the way, what is your name?"

The old passenger replied, "Louis Pasteur."[10]

In this season, Jesus is perfectly able to reveal Himself to us: in our longings, our frustrations, and our anxieties. He would be Lord to those who allow Him to be. Bill Ratliff says, "I am convinced that it is possible to deal with the transitions in our lives in such a way that the changes will be not only good but transformational."[11]

If we listen to the voice of God, we can emerge from the mid-life more doctrinally sound and committed than when we entered.

QUESTIONS
1. List the factors that have shaped you spiritually?
2. What notions in my belief system have made turning forty

so threatening? So meaningful?

3. How do you define "neighbor"? Has that definition changed significantly?

4. Are you taking your life seriously? List some decisions you can make to accomplish this.

Chapter Six

LIFE IS HARD, BUT GOD IS GOOD

She is forty-six, and I wish nothing worse to
happen to any woman.
— Sir Arthur Wing Pinero

GOAL FOR FORTYSOMETHINGS: To survive life's
tragedies, indignities, and injustices.

Life is hard. By the time a single adult has reached forty, most
of us have long since lost our fascination with fairy tales and
the "and they all lived happily ever after" endings.

Bertha Munro taught foreign languages in public schools
and at a small church college in Rhode Island. Life was good
for the young scholar. She had a brilliant future.

Then in 1911, en route to Boston from Washington, D.C.
Miss Munro's train derailed, and she was pinned in the wreck-
age. Miraculously, Bertha escaped death but lived the rest of
her life with a crippled hand and injured back. In those hours
waiting to be rescued, she made a final commitment to a life's
work. Bertha decided that her life belonged to God in a special way. Would that special way include marriage? Only time
would tell.

Soon she joined the founding faculty of Eastern Nazarene college in Boston. In her own words, from 1919 on "the story of my life is in one sense the story of Eastern Nazarene College."[1] When she became Academic Dean, she balanced a heavy administrative load with teaching and counseling.

Meanwhile, she commuted across town to Harvard working on her Ph.D. Then life got hard. Harvard officials informed Miss Munro that her dissertation was being duplicated by a British scholar and would be published in book form in England before she could complete her degree; she would have to select another topic. This single adult, near exhaustion from the heavy academic load, and short of money, decided not to complete her doctorate. During those troublesome days, the phrase, "not somehow but triumphantly" rang in her heart.[2]

By today's success-oriented perspective, many would consider her decision a failure. Hardly. The decision freed Munro as a fortysomething to fully invest herself in building a first-class liberal arts college in the shadow of the nation's leading educational giants.

Miss Munro's life illustrates a principle a fortysomething needs to comprehend.

LIMITED IMMUNITY

"Life is hard. It's not fair!" I clearly remember my father's response to my protest, "We're not talking about fair. We are talking about life."

When Dr. Bernie Siegel, professor of surgery at Yale, one of the nations' leading cancer specialists, shares a diagnosis with a patient, he often hears an angry or anguished, "Why me? Why do I have cancer?"

After years of breaking bad news he now responds, "Because you are part of the human race." Rather than "Why me?" Dr. Siegel powerfully argues the question ought to be, "Why not me?"[3]

Unfortunately, some Christian leaders these days proclaim a gospel of immunity, "I'm a King's kid! The devil, cancer, or divorce has no authority over me!" This kind of theology makes me uncomfortable. A card I often send to hurting people has words by Paul Claudel: "Jesus did not come to explain away suffering or remove it. He came to fill it with His presence."

The simple truth is, bad things do happen to good people.

I first observed real suffering in watching my dad's degenerative battle with nephritis (kidney disease). It was first assumed that his type of nephritis was hereditary, meaning that I could eventually have the same malady. Why was my dad sick? He had not smoked, drank, or caroused in forty years. He had been a leading elder in our congregation. His wallet was always open to the church. My mother once demanded of me, "You are the one with the doctorate in religion. Answer me this: Why is God treating your father like this?"

I couldn't answer her question. I had too many questions of my own.

Simply, there is no limited immunity from the storms of life. Jesus, a single adult, said, "He causes His sun to rise on the evil and the good, and sends rain on the righteous and the unrighteous" (Matt. 5:45).

BALANCED EXPECTATIONS

Some single adults have a high degree of tolerance for tough conditions. My friend, Jerry Traylor has run the New York Marathon, up Pike's Peak and across the United States — 3,500 miles.

So what?

He ran it on crutches!

Jerry was born with cerebral palsy and had gone through over a dozen corrective operations by the time he reached adolescence. Few people encouraged Jerry. When he finally was finished with body casts and steel leg braces, someone warned him, "Don't overdo it. Respect the limits of a cripple."

Jerry, a motivational speaker, often talks about his crutches, "There are two kinds of crutches — positive and negative. Mine are positive crutches. They help me, support me, and free me to get out and live life. But crutches can be negative, too, if people think that they are and let the crutches limit them or handicap them."[4]

Jerry doesn't have unrealistic expectations—he will never be a placekicker for the Chicago Bears. But he does have *balanced* expectations. When he ran his "Trail of New Beginnings" from San Francisco to New York, he knew that it would take him longer than other runners; he could barely average fifteen miles a day. But that meant that he was fifteen miles closer to New York than the day before.

Admittedly, some friends, tried to talk him out of it. He experienced some pretty discouraging moments. But he persevered, "not somehow but triumphantly."

Jerry tells audiences, "I don't think anything I do is really that remarkable. What's remarkable is life . . . What I do is just to live life and make the best of every single thing the Lord has given me to use. So long as I keep trying, I don't worry about falling down."[5]

Fortysomethings need balanced expectations.

FAIR COMPARISONS

Growing up at my house was tough. At times I was afraid to close both eyes during prayer or I might lose my piece of chicken. My parents had to listen to a steady stream of "He got a bigger piece than I did." "He got more." But that was understandable, we were children.

Many days, all the Lord hears from us is whining. Many fortysomethings have a litany that begins like this: "If only my _____ were _____, then I would be happy/married/contented." And I can whine with the best of them.

I have long had a battle of comparing myself to others. If I just had a lot of hair, or perfect teeth, or a more athletic torso. Such comparisons are common in our body beautiful world. Studies even show that elementary school children make friends based on "attraction."

I was wounded by the intense comparisons that began in the locker rooms of junior high school, when adolescent development was not uniform. Males don't have the freedom to freely verbalize the physical comparisons—except to tease.

That, in turn, only heightened the impact. We cannot laugh off the comparisons, especially the ones linked to sexuality. And everyone wonders why teenage suicide is so rampant. It didn't matter that I was a member of the Chess Club, Debate Team, and had a 3.4 grade point average. I was a nerd to the teens of my church.

Females suffer because of our society's fixation with the bosom. What begins as teasing in junior high, becomes open admiration in high school and society. Americans want to know Miss America's measurements. However, this fascination with breasts wounds a lot of young women, perhaps for a lifetime if they do not measure up—especially in families that engaged in much teasing. During the teen years a woman with only modest breast development has to come to terms with the potential scarring through men's comments, stares, and actions.

At the beach and by the pool, even Christian men notice physical endowment. We don't have to say anything. Our look gives away the thought: "Did you get a load of that!" Many single men act as if that particular body part were the sum total of the person.

Physical comparisons are kept before us by the constant barrage of TV commercials asking, "You know what the problem with your body is?" They promise, "Use our product and life will be different." So single adults race to buy all sorts of potions and lotions to smear on, dab on, spray on, or roll on their imperfect bodies.

I often wish that I could have interviewed some of the single adults profiled in this book. I have thought that they were lucky to have lived before the body beautiful craze. What would Henrietta Mears or Dietrich Bonhoeffer have thought about our culture's obsession with sexual attractiveness? I think that the reactions of these two saints would be obvious.

When was the last time you stood naked after a shower and took a good look at your body? I am afraid to. I know where the weight is. I know why I can no longer wear size thirty-six slacks. It is only a short step to demanding of the mirror,

"Who would ever find *this* body attractive?"
I especially feel ill at ease at the health club. Macho hunks
are everywhere, although I suspect it is the guys like me that
pay the overhead and keep the lights on. I can sweat myself
into a mess but I will never look like they do! Never.

Because of our anti-body attitudes, we sometimes say
"yeses" sexually that are not in our own best interest, let
alone the will of God. Fortysomething women admit that if
they aren't permissive many men won't call back. And the
competition is stiff—especially from young women. One
fortysomething told a female friend of mine, "Honey, here's
my number. Call me when you change your mind."

In our body conscious society, we look at people and make
immediate comparisons: her X is better/bigger/more developed than mine, rather than getting to know the person inside
the body.

Comparing leads to coveting. That's why Moses got so specific: "You shall not covet . . . anything that is your neighbor's" (Ex. 20:17, NKJV). Isaiah wrote something that I believe
can liberate us: "He [Jesus] had no beauty or majesty to
attract us to Him, nothing in His appearance that we should
desire Him" (Isa. 53:2). Jesus can understand my negative
feelings about my body and your feelings about yours.

I need to come to terms with the prophet's verse because I
have overvalued physical attraction. I have hurt people in dat-
ing and in friendships because I have rated physical appearance high on my priority scale. My attitude is sinful. I, like so
many other fortysomethings, have missed out on getting to
know some incredible people because I have been too concerned with the packaging.

Fortysomethings need to rediscover that there is more to
people than looks. We have brains, hearts, sensitivities, wonderful senses of humor, and imaginations too. Don't those
count? Oh yes! Why waste any more time grieving about yesterday's body? I intend to do the best with today's body. I
intend to listen to Jesus' words, "Do not worry . . . about your
body" (Matt. 6:25) so that I can "seek first His kingdom, and
His righteousness" (Matt. 6:33).

A COMMITMENT TO HEALING

At age forty-three I need healing. To look at me you might say, "From what? You've got a beautiful home, a career, recognition, a good car, art, savings." Yes, but those are the dimensions of me I want you to see.

I sat at lunch recently with a writer/minister that I respect. We had had a wonderful meal during which I shared frustration about my writing career. After carefully listening to my lament for some time, he leaned forward and spoke.

"Hank," — he is the only person who calls me by a nickname — "I miss the old you."

I looked puzzled.

"Let me explain. I remember the old Harold, who was vulnerable, who just stood naked in front of the world in the book *Jason Loves Jane.* Even though I had not yet met you after reading that book, I felt like I knew you." He paused.

"But lately, I read your books, and I can't find Hank. I find one who is observant but detached. Professional. Aloof. Your books now are filled with footnotes and stories about other people. But no Hank."

I started to protest but stopped, I knew that God had arranged this conversation for my benefit.

"Give us some Hank. *Please.* Forget the best-sellers and what X, Y and Z are writing and selling. Let me listen to your heartbeat. I am just as scared of mid-life as you are. I need to know someone is as scared as I am. I don't need answers and formulas and easy one-two-threes. I need to know that I am not the only one going through all this."

That conversation upset the applecart of my planned research approach for writing this book. Long after lunch, my friend's words were ricocheting up and down the canyons of my heart. As a result, I have become more transparent in writing and speaking. I don't have the map totally figured out.

I reached age forty-three with a backpack stuffed with wounds, hurts, regrets. Some authors call it "the shadow" — that part of our personality that we are afraid of or that we have ignored. Robert Bly calls it, "The long bag we drag behind us. We spend our life until we're twenty deciding what parts of ourselves to put into the bag, and we spend the rest of our lives trying to get them out again."⁶ The bag only gets heavier and heavier to drag. A mid-life crisis like the death of a spouse or a divorce may result in the bag being ripped or the contents being dumped out for all to see.

I frequently go back and reread the following passage that I discovered in 1977. Authentic living, Sidney Jourard said,

> . . . is risky. The chief risk lies in letting other people know how one has experienced the events impinging on one's life. All that other people can ever see of an individual is the expurgated version he discloses through his actions. A man's public utterances are often radically different from what he authentically feels and believes. Many of us dread to be known by others as intimately as we know ourselves [and as God knows us] because we would be divorced, fired, imprisoned, or shot.⁷

Jourard added, "Loving is scary" because when someone knows where to put the balm to heal you, they know where to drop the bomb to destroy you!⁸ By mid-life, most of us have bags filled with things we've never been able to tell a soul.

Through God's grace to me, I am a busy speaker. But the responsibility that goes with that privilege is enormous. I feel that *every* time I speak I have to deliver the goods. And sometimes I am tired, lonely, depressed, or defeated spiritually. Sometimes, I cannot say that singleness is wonderful!

There is a little boy in me that was not nourished as a child. Now, at forty-three, I have been forced to admit the little guy's presence. He wants to be loved. He wants to be recognized. He wants to be himself.

My heart has never completely healed after my divorce. In fact, despite all my friends and colleagues who do divorce recovery programs, I question if there is ever really a *complete* healing.

In my early days post divorce, I was on the defensive, at least in some Christian quarters. It is as if divorce is on one side of the scale, and I have tried to put enough "good" things on the other side to balance it.

Now in my forties, it's time to lighten the backpack and put away the scales. I cannot carry around all this emotional garbage. I need to be free of the bag and the scales. I have begun to understand grace in my forties, as unmerited grace that Jesus offers. It is second chances . . . and more. God bends low to touch us through His Son in this sometimes "upside down" season.

My friend Steve Shoemaker explained, "God is redeeming the world [and individuals] through the astounding power of grace!"[9] But grace requires that we own up to our needs.

In the last chapter, I mentioned my appreciation for J.B. Phillips' New Testament translation. Listen to my paraphrase of 1 John 1:8-10: "If we refuse to admit *that we need healing*, then we live in a world of illusion and truth becomes a stranger to us. But if we freely admit that we *need healing*, we find God utterly reliable and straightforward—He *heals* us and makes us thoroughly clean from all that is evil. For if we take the attitude *we do not need healing* we deny God's diagnosis of our condition and cut ourselves off from what He had to say to us."

Someone has said, "In love He made us, in love He will mend us." I agree.

A biblical personality, Esau, illustrates these principles. He did not marry until he was forty (Gen. 26:34); apparently he tried to make up for lost time by marrying two wives, Judith and Basemath, who were a source of grief to his parents, Isaac and Rebekah.

Genesis 27 focuses on Jacob's scheme to steal his father's blessing (with generous assistance from his mother). Jacob—a man with smooth skin and aware of his father's failing eyesight—covered his arms with goatskins to simulate his brother Esau's hairiness.

Isaac hesitated to bestow the blessing, "The voice is the voice of Jacob, but the hands are the hands of Esau" (v. 22). He asked, "Are you really my son Esau?" (v. 24)

Jacob lied, "I am" (v. 24).

So, Isaac blessed the younger son. Esau arrived soon thereafter with game for his father's meal. In an instant, the tired old father realized he had been tricked. He moaned, "I ate it just before you came and I blessed him — and indeed he will be blessed" (v. 33).

Esau, burst out with a loud and bitter cry, "Bless me — me too, my father!" (v. 34)

All Isaac could say was, "Your brother came deceitfully and took your blessing" (v. 35).

The encounter between the disappointed son and the deceived father is heart wrenching. Esau asked, "Haven't you reserved any blessing for me? Do you have only one blessing, my father? Bless me too!" (vv. 36, 38)

There was no immunity that day for Esau. No instant replay. He had been done in by his twin brother and by his mother.

How did this fortysomething react? "Esau held a grudge against Jacob because of the blessing his father had given him (v. 41). And I suspect toward his father: How could he have been tricked? Esau reasoned, "The days of mourning for my father are near; then I will kill my brother Jacob" (v. 41).

Momma got involved, afraid that her fair-haired Jacob would be done in. She warned Jacob, "Your brother Esau is consoling himself with the thought of killing you" (v. 42). Apparently, Rebekah didn't think that would come to pass because she told Jacob, "When you brother is no longer angry with you and forgets what you [not we] did to him, [How could he forget?] I'll send word for you to come back from there" (v. 45).

Rebekah knew that she had lost her relationship with Esau, through her interference, when she said, "Why should I lose both of you in one day?" (v. 45)

After this, the fortysomething named Jacob — now the blessed one — set out for the land of Haran where he would learn a thing or two about being forty and single.

A BREATHING SPACE

Fortysomethings need a breathing space, a port in which to weather the storm. When too many things are changing and changing too rapidly, we need safe places. I am grateful to Gordon MacDonald for developing this theme in his book *Restoring Your Spiritual Passion.* "We need safe places in our world. Not merely when we are in trouble but when we need to rest a bit, to regain our measure of spiritual passion and composure for the continuing challenges of the cue balls that constantly come at us."[10]

My experience has been just about the time you have the forties figured out, you get smacked with a cue ball and are sent reeling.

But MacDonald added, "Moreover, the biographical maps of holy men and women are marked with countless rectangles: the places they made safe by meeting Christ there. Or should I say, the places Christ made safe by meeting them there?"[11]

We find Jacob making camp at Bethel, a breathing space. That night God visited this fortysomthing on the run from his brother's anger. God promised:

I am the Lord the God of your father Abraham and the God of Isaac. I will give you and your descendants the land on which you are lying. Your descendants will be like the dust of the earth, and you will spread out to the west and to the east, to the north and to the south. All people on earth will be blessed through you and your offspring. I am with you and will watch over you wherever you go, and I will bring you back to this land. I will not leave you until I have done what I have promised you (Gen. 28:13-15).

What a promise! If Jacob had listened he would have heard: "you and your descendants" "your descendants" and "through you and your offspring." And since he had zero offspring at that moment, he could have deduced that he was going to survive his brother's wrath.

Jacob—upon awakening—blustered, "Surely the Lord is in this place, and I was not aware of it" (Gen. 28:16).

What about this place you find yourself in—your Bethel equivalent? Can you repeat Jacob's words? So many forty-somethings are demanding, "God, where are You in the midst of my crisis?" He is there. The problem is that we cannot recognize His presence. God does not comply with our preconceived notions about timing.

All of us need our Bethels. Breathing places. Places where we too can hear with our own ears, "I will not leave you until I have done for you what I have promised you" (Gen. 28:15).

Profile of a Fortysomething: Barbara Jordan (1936–   ). Politician and professor. In the summer of 1974, this single adult was sitting on the House Judiciary Committee weighing the evidence in the impeachment proceedings of Richard M. Nixon, President of the United States. There were varied opinions on the committee, but many people listened carefully when Barbara Jordan spoke. Bruce Morton of CBS News labeled her, "the best mind on the committee."

The daughter of a black Houston clergyman, Barbara had always wanted to do something unusual. "I never wanted to be run-of-the-mill." For a while she thought she might be a pharmacist. "But then I thought, whoever heard of an outstanding pharmacist?" Her life changed when she heard a black woman lawyer speak at school.

By 1959, Barbara Jordan had a reputation as a spellbinding orator, a law degree from Boston University, and had passed the Texas and Massachusetts bar exams. Her first law office was at her mother's dining room table.

In 1960 she worked hard in Houston for the Kennedy-Johnson ticket; she ran for the state house but lost although 46,000 people voted for her. "I figured anybody who could get 46,000 people to vote for them for any office should keep on trying." Defeated again, she could have grumbled, what can a black woman in Texas expect? But in 1955, Barbara ran for the state Senate, and became the first black woman ever elected in the state.

What was next? Some counseled her not to set her expectations too high and to enjoy her "safe" seat. In 1972 she ran for Congress on the pledge, "I can get things done." Although Barbara had no spouse to stand beside her and pose for "family pictures" or to serve coffee, Miss Jordan had a reputation and a power for oratory. She won her seat by 66,000 votes!

Perhaps some counseled her that she would now have difficulty finding a man. Barbara never ruled out marriage but noted, "Politics is almost totally consuming. . . . A good marriage requires that one attend to it and not treat it as another hobby."

Through media exposure during Watergate, and then through her powerful address to the Democratic National Convention, covered by the three major networks during prime time, millions leaned forward and asked, "Who is this woman?"

There was even talk that someday this single could be a Democratic vice presidential candidate, until she announced she would not run for reelection and accepted a professorship at the University of Texas. Veteran politicians wondered what was going on.

As a fortysomething, she turned her back on politics and walked away from all she had struggled to accumulate. Barbara wanted a breathing place.

She had been diagnosed as having a degenerative bone disease. Barbara Jordan chose to retire from the pressures of public office to maximize her resources and strength. Now confined to a wheelchair, she kept the diagnosis from many people rather than be pitied.

Today, as a professor at the University of Texas, Miss Jordan is still a positive role model of a fortysomething woman. Although she sits in a wheelchair, she personifies Miss Munro's proverb, "not somehow but triumphantly!" But the mind, voice, and especially the spirit have not been diminished. A classroom offers her an invaluable safe place to make a difference to the next generation of this country's political leaders. And in occasional speeches across the country, she still demonstrates a gifted oratorical style that wins standing ovations.[12]

Life's tragedies, indignities and injustices are meant to be survived. Why did this illness strike Barbara Jordan? I don't know. But I do value her example as a single adult who is a survivor.

CONCLUSION

Life is hard, there is no doubt about that! In light of that reality, our task as fortysomethings is to survive life's tragedies, indignities, and injustices. We need to recognize our vulnerability. Why things happen is the core mystery of life — married fortysomethings have no more "answers" than single adults. As fortysomethings, we have only limited immunity. We need to balance our expectations. We need to make fair comparisons, alert to the fact that comparisons lead to coveting. Finally, we need to establish and maintain "breathing spaces" or places where we can weather the "I can't believe this is happening to me!" events of life.

QUESTIONS

1. What is the worst thing that could happen to you?
2. In what ways has life "gotten hard" for you?
3. Has your past been a tutor or a resource pool? What lessons have you learned from life's hardness?
4. What are you "coveting"?

Chapter Seven

MARCHING OFF THE MAP

*Then, for the first time in my life, I reflected
on my past and cursed all my deeds and the
fifty years that I would shortly attain:
O horror! with the weight of forty-seven
years upon me. . . . In my old
age I find no pleasure save in the memories
which I have of the past.*

— *Casanova*

**GOAL FOR FORTYSOMETHINGS: To stretch
my boundaries.**

Alexander the Great wept when he reached the point of discovering there were no more kingdoms for him to conquer. He had marched to the edge of the map.

Not all of Alexander's colleagues got as far as he did. Indeed, some were limited by the maps they used. In those days, ancient mapmakers wrote this proclamation at the edge of the maps: "Beyond this point there be dragons!"

Many fortysomethings are looking at maps that say the same thing. I received one birthday card that suggested, "From here on out . . . it's downhill all the way." Says who?

I am not where I wanted to be professionally at forty-three. I have written more than twenty books and have had no bestseller. I can walk into many Christian bookstores and not find any of my books. I have spent hundreds of hours mulling over the whys. If only I had a radio show, or a TV ministry, or a full-time publicist. I know that God is my source. But my plans, my wishes, my career expectations keep getting in the way.

Perhaps by forty, you may have missed some promotions that you thought were in the bag. You have had to stand in the crowd while another less qualified person is honored. It hurts.

As I was writing this, I received a note from my friend Dwayne who has listened to my "wound." He wrote, "I ran across this and thought of you":

We mostly spend [our] lives conjugating three verbs: to Want, to Have, and to Do. Craving, clutching, and fussing . . . we are kept in perpetual unrest: forgetting that none of these verbs have any ultimate significance, except so far as they are transcended by and included in, the fundamental verb, to Be: and that Being, not wanting, having and doing, is the essence of a spiritual life.[1]

But with Dwayne's scrawl, I thought the quote read, "that Being, *not writing* . . . is the essence of a spiritual life." That quote tore through my heart like a well-aimed arrow. If only I had spent as much time nurturing my heart as I had in conjugating *want-have-achieve-accomplish-write* I would be experiencing a richer, more meaningful mid-life. I have discovered that I have been living in a desert, spiritually and emotionally.

Henri Nouwen says "as long as we have only a vague inner feeling of discontent with our present way of living, and only an indefinite desire for 'things spiritual' our lives will continue to stagnate in a generalized melancholy."[2] Unfortunately, too many fortysomethings get used to the discontent. Such an attitude prevents us from actively seeking the Architect who could draw us a blueprint for a richer way of living. In essence we settle for crumbs rather than the banquet entrée.

"Our first task," Nouwen points out, "is to dispel the vague, murky feeling of discontent and to look critically at how we are living our lives."[3] We dare to ask God to turn up the heat on our discontent from a low grade fever, as Daniel Taylor suggests, to a full boil. Taylor confronted me on this issue:

> Rather than a mid-life crisis, I have probably had a low-grade fever on this issue since I was really quite young. I don't expect it to go away, and perhaps it shouldn't. People have undoubtedly pointed out to you that the author of twenty-two books, best-sellers or not, has almost inevitably made a difference in people's lives and therefore in the eternal scheme of things. But I think I agree with you that "on the bad days" as you say, that fact doesn't carry much force.
>
> For me, what is much more important is what I take to be a promise from God that if I seek to live my life by His principles, He will guarantee that my life has meaning, now and forever. I can't point directly to the Bible verse that says that, but I have no doubt that it's so.
>
> So, while it is not likely, your "bad days" fears may prove correct. Maybe none of the many books you write will "last." But I think God has guaranteed that the effect of a life spent in even partial service to eternal values *will* last. And that's more amazing than we can comprehend.[4]

Apparently a lot of fortysomethings are wandering through the desert. I have treasured Daniel Taylor's letter to me for its opening words. "I of course know exactly what you are talking about regarding your mid-life crisis." I didn't need a translator. He understood.

I was struck by one yuppie lawyer who wrote, "I have simply come to the point of despair. My mind refuses to think and I am not able to cope." He composed those words just before jumping off the Golden Gate Bridge to his death.[5]

Some suspect that he, like so many of us fortysomethings, suffered from "winner blues." A feeling that despite great success and achievement, despite our press clippings, and plaques on the walls, we are inadequate. There is an ache in our hearts that we cannot silence or fill. There's got to be more than accumulating wealth or possessions.

For some of us, any setback is unbearable. Time is moving too quickly. Look at your appointment books. We preface many requests with "I *know* you're busy, but this will only take a minute." We live our life in one-minute segments.

Perhaps just merely marking time in the same position — despite pay raises or bonuses or security — is driving you crazy. You have a game plan to the top. You have to get it while you can or before someone else gets there. Our generation has defied upward mobility and impoverished our souls in the process. But when do we find time to care for our hearts?

Therapist Barbara Kolenda said, "Everybody is supposed to be making it and loving it, so when people get successful, it stops being fun because they have to work so hard to maintain it."[6]

Look at the insanity of our weekends. Packed with lists of "to do" items, places to be, and things to do and see and experience. One pastor told me, "I have a feeling most of my congregation are en route somewhere on Sunday morning. Worship is not the highlight of the day — it is merely another thing to get done before sunset."

No wonder JoAnne Martin from Stanford University Business School predicts the onslaught of a massive wave of mid-career crises during the nineties among those fortysomethings who wanted "more" but settled for less. Who will be the first in your group of friends to say "enough"?[7]

WAYS TO DO SOMETHING ABOUT THE MAP
Fortunately, for the fortysomethings, we live in an age of great programs, organizations, and resources to help us reread and redraw the map.

When I was a little boy I thought Dad was the smartest man in the world. In a strange town, he always knew which road to take to get us where we were going. I marveled at his ability to get us through some of those intersections.

I have never forgotten the day in Vincennes, Indiana when he pulled to the side of the road and pointed to the road signs. He gave me a lesson in navigation. There were U.S. and state roads, both identified by signs. All one had to do was to look for and follow the signs. The signs had been there all along. I just didn't know how to look for them. That's true in life as well.

But how can we begin to "reread" the maps?

GO BACK TO SCHOOL

I remember the day I received my master's degree, my dad asked, "What's next?" When I answered doctoral work, my mother responded, "Are you sure you need more education?"

Education is a lifelong journey. While I have a string of little letters behind my name, there is so much more I want to learn. For example, I am looking into two programs called the Master of Liberal Arts. The programs are designed for people like me who slept through English Literature 201 or World Civilization 101. Those first two years of college my intellect never got warmed up. I was concerned only with what I had to know to pass the final exam and get my C.

Today, going back to school could mean taking some courses at a junior college. Anything and everything from Cake Decorating 101 to Accounting 102 is offered. In fact, some singles take courses as a way to meet other singles.

Clarice Zureick attended her daughter's graduation at Kentucky's Berea College. Clarice didn't sit with the other parents, she sat *beside* her daughter. Both were awarded bachelor's degrees at the 1990 commencement. After she encouraged her daughter Amy to attend, this single parent dusted off her old dream and matriculated as well.

She said, "I thought if I don't do it now, I wouldn't go. So, I gave a year's notice at my job and did it."[8]

Unless you live in an isolated area, there are incredible educational opportunities near you. And in the future more schools will be bringing education to you through satellite courses taught at night in a local high school or church. Hundreds of fortysomethings are enrolled in Liberty University's School of Lifelong Learning, taking advantage of "long-distance" instruction through their VCRs both at undergraduate and graduate levels.

Check out the educational opportunities in your area. Nourish your fortysomething brain!

READ

The person who *does* not read has little advantage over the person who *cannot* read. I was stunned by the August 1989 issue of *Personnel Administrator*. In bold 1½ inch letters on the cover I read, "27 MILLION AMERICANS CANNOT READ THIS." The issue of the journal focused on workplace illiteracy.[9]

How well do you read? Some single adults are keeping a deep, dark secret from their friends and family members. They cannot read or are dissatisfied with their level of reading comprehension. Others claim they do not have time or are too tired.

In an information age, reading skills make or break you. Complex training manuals and employee handbooks require above-average reading and comprehension skills. So do leases, contracts, repair manuals, and legal agreements with that infamous fine print.

Some of us read slowly. One of my goals for my forties is to take a speed reading course, just to keep up with the "have to" reading. Many of you work in jobs or professions where hundreds of pages of letters, memos, or reports cross your desk every week. How do you read it all?

1. *It is important to read widely.* One troublesome area is spiritual and intellectual reading. Many do not read critically. We practice bathroom reading that requires little imagination or wrestling with words and concepts. It has no lasting impact. We imbibe junk books along with our junk food. No wonder we're malnourished intellectually.

Dennis Kinlaw has made a distinction between being *well-read* and *read well* in a remarkable article, "Don't Ever Read a Good Book!" He recounted chauffeuring theologian A.W. Tozer. As a student, Kinlaw took advantage of the opportunity to quiz the scholar about his reading habits. Tozer said, "Don't ever read a good book. . . . You don't have time. If there is a better book on the subject for goodness' sake don't

read the good one! . . . Kinlaw, there is a difference between
having read widely and having read well. I would much rather
be well-read than widely read. That is why I often reread an
old work rather than reach for a new one. If it is a great book,
it deserves more than one reading."

After being with Tozer, Kinlaw admitted, "I was conscious
of how much of my reading hardly merited the description
'good' to say nothing of 'best.' " He said, "my criteria for
reading were affected that day."[10]

I have thanked God across the years for friends like Sara,
Elva, Ilona, Michael, Jim, Carole, Stephen, and Bev for book
recommendations. Their postcards saying, "You've *got* to read
_____ " are taken seriously. Recommending books is an
important ministry. After all the *right* book at the *right* time
with the *right* reader can make a difference.

2. *It is important to read secularly.* I am concerned that the
Christian community is becoming an anti-intellectual ghetto.
Too many Christians have the idea if a book is not found in a
Christian bookstore it should not be read. As a result, many
people are missing some great ideas and practical insights.

3. *It is important to read deliberately.* Today, books have to
compete with VCRs, cable TV, fatigue, and the temptation to
invest ourselves in the sensational. I am concerned about the
"airport fiction" that so many single adults consider literature
(sex and violence every 2.3 pages). I know single adults who
would picket adult book stores but have stacks of "bodice
rippers" romance novels on their nightstands. Paul advised,
"Whatever is true, whatever is noble, whatever is right, whatever is pure, whatever is lovely, whatever is admirable . . .
think [read] about such things" (Phil. 4:8).

4. *It is important to reread.* Dr. Elton Trueblood, the great
Quaker writer-scholar, had commented on his reading in retirement. "Now, at last, I have the time [to read]. I realize
that we tend to read the great books too early, before we have
enough experience to understand them, and sometimes we
never open them again. Such neglect is a serious mistake,
which may be corrected."[11]

Remember *Cliff Notes?* Now is the time to go back and read

94 Fortysomething and Single

the original. One commitment I have made for the nineties is to read ninety classics. Why? In high school and college, if a book contained anything I considered "unchristian" I refused to read it.

As a fortysomething, I have written friends who are avid readers and asked for "lists" of classics and their recommendations. A librarian suggested I read *The Lifetime Reading Plan*—an introduction to more than one hundred classics of Western thought—written by Clifton Fadiman, a member of the Board of Editors of the *Encyclopedia Britannica* and the Book of the Month Club. Fadiman concedes it "may take you fifty years to finish" his list but the reading will be "a source of continuous growth."[12] (See Appendix for suggestions.) The Plan was designed "to help us avoid mental bankruptcy" and is "meant for Americans . . . who are curious to see what their minds can master in the course of their remaining lifetime."[13]

TRAVEL

My father, in seventy-six years of his life, visited ten states. Some months traveling alone I'm in ten states. I remember as a child getting all those "Having a good time, wish you were here" postcards. I stared at the pictures for hours, wishing. I decided to make travel a priority in my life. As a result, I now *send* "Wish you were here" postcards.

I remember getting down on my knees on top of the Great Wall of China to thank God for allowing me to be there. The little boy in me danced joyously in the rain, soaking up every minute of the experience. I felt the same way standing in front of the Pyramids . . . at the Vatican . . . at Buckingham Palace . . . at the Wailing Wall.

Yes, international travel costs money. I could only afford it by driving a VW, without a heater or radio, until it was 15 years old and had 125,000 miles on it. Some of my friend's priorities included new cars. I preferred to stretch my world through travel.

One single friend of mine has an incredible plan. Every year at spring break he picks two neighboring states. He flies to the first state, rents a car and then "sees" the state, from its big cities to the small hamlets. He gets off the interstates and cruises down country roads. His goal is to tour every state capital and capitol. He knows more about some states than many of their residents. Sure, it's going to take a quarter of a century to complete his plan, but he's committed.

Henrietta Mears loved to travel. One day she found herself at the Taj Mahal in India. The tour guide, to demonstrate the acoustics of "a wonder of the world," stepped onto a little platform and shouted: "There is no God but Allah and Mohammed is his prophet!" The words echoed down the marbled halls.

Vacation or no, the challenge was too much for the single adult from Hollywood. "May I try that?" she asked. With the guide's permission, she stepped up on the platform, took a deep breath and thundered, "Jesus Christ, Son of God, is Lord over all!" Like a volley of rifle fire, her words echoed until she assured the guide he could now continue the tour.

Henrietta Mears "hiked rhino-infested jungles in Africa, climbed mountains in Formosa, and walked amid the dying in India—all in order to obtain a better world view—to clarify the vision God put in her heart to reach a world with the Gospel of Jesus Christ."[14]

VOLUNTEER

A good cure for the "poor me" syndrome is volunteering. Management specialist, Peter Drucker, notes that every other adult—a total of 80 million Americans—works as a volunteer, giving an average of nearly five hours each week to one or more organizations. If these volunteers were paid, their pay—even calculated at minimum wage would be $150 billion a year.[15]

Profile of a Fortysomething: Dorothea Lynde Dix (1802–1887). American social reformer. Dorothea had been snubbed by much of the elite of Boston society, despite her brilliance. At age twenty-two she had published an elementary science textbook; at age twenty-

nine, a hymnbook for children and several devotional and
poetry books. Life was hard for her. She had had a broken engagement and then developed tuberculosis. She
couldn't teach because of her fragile health and lived off
a small inheritance from her grandmother.

Then in March, 1841, a Harvard divinity student
asked her to substitute teach a Sunday School class for
women at the Cambridge jail. She had no indication as
she walked in the cold that morning that she was facing a
turning point.

At the jail, she found foul, bare, unheated quarters for
the women. Moreover, she was shocked to find the in-
sane housed with drunks, vagrants, prostitutes, and hard-
ened criminals. When she told the jailer that they were
cold, he laughed, "Oh, Miss Dix, crazy folks don't feel
the cold."

Dorothea snapped, "If I am cold, they are cold! *Get
them some heat!*" In those days, mental illness was such an
embarrassment to families, particularly among the poor
and uneducated, that they were hidden, locked in cages.
Out of sight, out of mind. But not to Dorothea.

With the encouragement of Boston philanthropist
Samuel Gridley Howe, Miss Dix launched an intensive
eighteen month investigation into the care of the mentally ill that resulted in a shocking public indictment
before the Massachusetts legislature in January, 1843.
With power, Miss Dix described her discovery of human
beings: "confined in cages, closets, cellars, stalls, pens!
Chained, naked, beaten with rods, lashed into obedience."

"I come to place before the Legislature of Massachusetts the condition of the miserable, the desolate, the
outcast" she declared without hesitation. Because of this
fortysomething's tenacity and her rigorous documenta-
tion, the legislature initiated reform.

This fortysomething didn't go back to her garden and
ladies teas with the literary society. Dorothea Dix went
on to Rhode Island, then New York, and on to New

Jersey where she helped establish that state's first mental hospital, a facility she called, "my firstborn child."

From 1844 to 1847, Dix traveled 30,000 miles from Pennsylvania to Alabama, conducting investigations and petitioning legislatures for reform. Eventually, this fortysomething's name became a household word for compassion. As a volunteer, she shamed this country into a more human care for the mentally ill.

With the outbreak of the Civil War, Miss Dix volunteered for service. On June 10, 1861, she was named superintendent of nurses for the Union Army. She opened infirmaries, trained and recruited nurses, stockpiled medical supplies, and took on more than her fair share of bureaucratic battles. But, as a result of her work, nursing became an accepted profession for women, and thousands of men survived battlefield wounds.

Both endeavors were volunteer posts. Few women have left such a mark on American culture as Dorothea Dix.

President Millard Fillmore once remarked to her, "It is strange to me, how you find time to accomplish everything and especially everything good."

How did a single woman answer the President of the United States? "God requires no more to be accomplished than He gives time for performing."[16]

At Christmastime, many single adults place Christmas seals on their Christmas cards with little awareness of the fact that a forty-six-year-old single adult, Emily Bissell, initiated the tradition in this country.

Emily was a socialite in Wilmington, Delaware. Her interest in social concerns was stimulated by a Sunday School teacher who asked Emily to accompany her on visits to the homes of needy persons. Emily helped found the West End Reading Room, which sponsored Wilmington's first free kindergarten, as well as a program that was a forerunner of the Boy Scouts.

In the early 1900's, tuberculosis was a communicable disease and leading killer. Her cousin, Dr. Joseph P. Wales asked Emily to volunteer at a little "tuberculosis shack" he had built. Something more had to be done to save lives and end the suffering of the families.

Something from Emily's reading provided the answer. She had read that the Danish government had issued "Christmas stamps" to raise money to fight TB. If it worked there, it would work in Wilmington.

She obtained permission from the American Red Cross to use its seal, and through a group of volunteers sold the first American Christmas seals on December 7, 1907. The first year in the Wilmington and Philadelphia post offices, she and her volunteers made about $3,000. The next year she obtained the assistance of another single adult, Mabel Boardman of the American Red Cross, and a national campaign raised $135,000.

For forty years Miss Bissell gave herself to the fight against tuberculosis.[17]

Today there is no shortage of institutions, causes, and programs that could use volunteers. This is a time for single adults to lead the way. You may discover, as do most volunteers, that you get more out of it than you give.

CONCLUSION

The trials of Job are legendary. He had lost everything except his faith. Yet in all his calamity, "Job did not sin in what he said" (Job 2:10). Forty chapters later this statement appears: "The Lord blessed *the latter part* of Job's life more than the first" (Job 42:12, emphasis mine).

Your latter part can be the best too if you are willing to march off the map. Casanova may have had no pleasures except the memories of his past. But for the single adult who honors God it is always morning. And you don't need a license to make a difference.

Poor Alexander the Great. His fear of "the dragons" kept him from new worlds. There are always new things to learn, to experience, to smell, to taste, to touch — new kingdoms just beyond the bend. And as for the dragons, they're wimps.

Regardless of the experiences that have brought you to this point — fortysomething and single — the best is yet to be!

QUESTIONS
1. List the gifts/talents you have delayed developing.
2. What do you want to learn?
3. Does your reading impact your life? How?
4. What places do you want to experience through travel?
5. Read through Appendix C (see page 157). Place a check beside the books you haven't read. Select one and within forty-eight hours go to the library, check the work out, and read it.

Chapter Eight

BEYOND THIS POINT...
THERE BE DRAGONS!

I lately thought no man alive
Could ere improve past forty-five. . . .

"No Sir," says Johnson, "'tis not so,
'Tis your mistake, and I can show
An instant, if you doubt it,
You, who perhaps are forty-eight,
May still improve, 'tis not too late:
I wish you'd set about it . . . "
— Dr. Barnard, 1829

GOAL FOR FORTYSOMETHINGS: To create
opportunities today
that will become tomorrow's memories.

By mid-life most of us have some bad habits we keep to ourselves. After all, one fringe benefit of singleness and living alone is that you and your habits can keep each other company.

On my fortieth birthday I bought bathroom scales with easy to read numbers. Somehow, I had "blossomed" from 179 pounds to 228. I remember the moment I decided to do something about my weight. I had decided as a New Year's resolution to set up a program at my health club and stick to it.

I had to be weighed for the program charts. That day a gorgeous woman supervised the weigh-in. When I stepped on the scales I saw the "mm-hmm!" register on her face. Then she humiliated me by reciting the numbers aloud, as if I had not seen them.

I was pleased with my spiritual control. The only words that came out of my mouth were, "Oh?"

During my life, I have lost (and regained) a lot of weight. At my peak, I weighed 285 pounds and I carry a photo in my Daytimer to remind me of that time in my life. I lost weight through a diet, jogging, and regular workouts at the gym. How could I have allowed myself to balloon up again to 228?

Cherry nut ice cream. I found this wonderful treat at a neighborhood convenience store. On too many nights, I'd stretch out on my couch, turn on the stereo, and then let the cherry nut ice cream melt slightly before I spooned it down.

Since I was a single adult living alone I ate out of the carton. Most nights I didn't stop until the container was empty. I ate because I was lonely. Or frustrated. Or anxious. Or excited about a new idea. Or bored.

On Easter Sunday, 1989, at my church, I heard an announcement about the Overeaters Anonymous (O.A.) group's meeting. I knew the announcement was for me. O.A. met in the basement of the church on Thursday evenings at 7:30.

At 7:25, the next Thursday evening, I parked my car in the church parking lot. I waited until 7:29 ½. Finally, I opened the car door, dashed into the church meeting room, and sat down.

My heart was not beating as hard from the run as from the fear. I panicked. Afraid to look around the room, I sat with my eyes glued to the floor. I listened to the standard welcoming in O.A. Ironically, although I had done hundreds of single adult conferences, retreats, workshops—with as many as 7,000 people present—I was scared to death.

In O.A. you go around the group and, at least, introduce yourself. Most people then share something of their struggle. I was hoping that we would run out of time before it was my turn. Finally, the person next to me stopped and the group responded, "Thanks, Barb" and shifted their attention to me.

Although there were no spotlights or stage lights in that room—just the normal humming florescent lights—I would have sworn I was trapped in a sauna.

Without looking up, I mumbled, "My name is Harold . . . and I am a compulsive overeater." There, I had said it.

"Hi, Harold" they responded.

As I shared my stormy emotional pilgrimage to 228 pounds, these wonderful women and men listened. I rambled; I cried. I admitted that I ate when I was sexually frustrated. That I ate when I was lonely. I confessed that my eating habits were out of control. That sometimes after speaking to hundreds of single adults, I came back to a lonely motel room, found the snack machine, and exchanged my quarters for candy bars and snacks, which were really little chunks of comfort — caloric companions.

I admitted that although some single adults were afraid to eat out, alone, I relished it. That way I could eat as much as I wanted.

Also, as a speaker-writer, I am the recipient of gracious hospitality wherever I speak. At some of those meals, I ate like a squirrel storing up for a long, cold winter.

The group listened. No one interrupted. No one whispered. No one offered me any suggestions or easy one, two, three solutions.

When I finished my rambling, they said, as if on cue, in unison, "Thanks, Harold, for sharing."

At the end of the evening, we stood, held hands and repeated the Lord's Prayer. Although, I have to admit, that phrase, "Give us . . . our daily bread" sounded differently.

Then they said "Keep coming back! It works!"

I sneaked out of the room, got into my car and drove home. I was depressed and craving some caloric reward for my honesty. But I went back to another meeting. And I have kept going back, even when I have to report binges and failures. Through O.A. I have come to a startling conclusion: I am addicted to food, just like an alcoholic is addicted to alcohol. Only one difference: An alcoholic can live without alcohol. How am I supposed to live without food?

Oh, you protest, you just need some discipline. Get a hold of yourself and pray about it. But because of my particular

Christian upbringing, eating was the only permissable indulgence. Think how many church functions involve food? How can you have fellowship without food? "Fellowship" becomes synonymous with calories.

I have had to come to the point of admitting that *for me* overeating is sin.

Moreover, I have had to admit that I have not taken seriously the teaching that my body is the temple of the Holy Spirit (1 Cor. 6:12-20).

But, the good news is that as an overweight fortysomething, I don't have to continue this lifelong pattern. I can reverse my wrong attitudes on food and I can do something about the quiet resentment I have held toward those who can "really put it away" and never gain a pound.[1]

I have learned that any time I eat too much, or the wrong thing, I can ask God to intervene. Weakness says, "Well since you've broken your resolution, might as well go ahead and eat now. You can get a fresh start tomorrow."

No way. A fresh start begins *now!* That attitude is strengthened by a C.S. Lewis quotation:

Good and evil both increase at compound interest. That is why the little decisions you and I make every day are of such infinite importance. The smallest good act today is the capture of a strategic point from which, a few months later, you may be able to go on to victories you never dreamed of. And apparently trivial indulgence in lust or anger today is the loss of a ridge or railway line or bridgehead from which the enemy may launch an attack otherwise impossible.[2]

I don't go to O.A. to lose weight. I go to O.A. to find fresh encouragement. O.A. has a wonderful purpose: "Overeaters Anonymous is a fellowship of men and women who share their experiences, strength, and hope with each other that they may solve their common problem and help others to recover from compulsive overeating."[3]

I love that three point triangle of purpose: *experience, strength* and *hope*. That is exactly the kind of support that all fortysomethings need. With it we can gain the "victories" that C.S. Lewis discussed.

There are a lot of compulsions in "Singleland": sex, gambling, drinking, smoking, lying, shopping. And behind a lot of them is a sense of woundedness or lack of wholeness. "Addicted behavior patterns," Joseph Bailey argues, "are triggered at certain psychological temperatures of states of the mind"[4] — like dateless Friday nights when we compensate with a few thousand calories. This confirms what the proverbialist declared, "For as he thinketh in his heart, so is he" (Prov. 23:7, KJV). James Allen commented, "In the armory of thought he [humankind] forges the weapons by which he destroys himself; he also fashions the tools with which he builds for himself the heavenly mansions of joy and strength and peace."[5]

How about you? What dragons tempt you in your forties? This season is a wonderful time to confront the dragon and break some bad habits. Begin with this promise: "Commit to the Lord whatever you do, and your plans will succeed" (Prov. 16:3).

CELEBRATIONS

The parties don't have to stop at forty, even if the last one had all black decorations. Mid-life is not a prison sentence to be served with time off for good behavior. It is a celebration that mirrors the great celebration that is waiting for every believer, called eternity.

New Year's Eve is a tough time for a lot of single adults in the church. How much fun can it be to gather in the church fellowship hall, open some Fritos, and sing "Auld Lang Syne" and numerous verses of "Kumbaya"?

There is something about dressing up in tuxedos and gowns that appeals to many single adults. But they don't want to drink or try to fight for breath in a smoke-filled ballroom. They ask, "Why can't Christians have a first-class good time too?"

That's why I was so excited when a group of single adults in Detroit said, "Let's have a "Convivial Concrescence on New

Year's Eve!" What a celebration! There was great food, spectacular decorations, good music, comedy, and an inspirational talk on the decade ahead. We celebrated the end of a decade and the dazzling dawning of a new one ahead.

My friend Elva McAllaster, poet-in-residence at Greenville College, believes single adults need to celebrate more. In fact, she has proposed a "Doxology Day" for single adults. "What about," she asks, "each single's using his semi-annual birthday as his Doxology Day? That is, if you were born April 10, then on October 10 you and your friends could do the special praisings and celebratings."[6]

Think through this. You celebrate your married friends' showers and anniversaries. So why not celebrate a "Thank the Lord that you were born day!"

Maybe just by taking the day off, or going to the beach. Wherever or however it is a day to celebrate one's singleness. I can just hear the howls of protest!

- "I hate being single!"
- "I don't want attention drawn to my singleness!"
- "I'm not about to throw a hyprocritical party to celebrate what I hate, nor to praise God for being single!"

McAllaster admits that some "are free *not* to celebrate." While she understands the protesters, she reminds us that "The Christian way of life is to praise God *in all things.*"[7] Why?

1. *Praise is biblical.* "Bless the Lord, O my soul; and all that is within me, bless His holy name! Bless the Lord, O my soul, and forget not all His benefits" (Ps. 103:1-2, NKJV). That's the psalmist's way of saying, when you consider the alternatives, singleness is not so bad. The last verse of that psalm, says, "Bless the Lord, all His works, in all places of His dominion" (v. 22). If He really is Lord of all, then He has dominion over your singleness, too.

2. *Praise is traditional.* Our forefathers in the faith sang a wonderful Gospel song, "Count Your Blessings:" "When upon life's billows you are tempest tossed; When you are discouraged, thinking all is lost; Count your many blessing, name them one by one; And it will surprise you what the Lord hath done." When was the last time you counted your blessings?

You may be wondering if you have any. Consider Paul, a single adult who had been beaten, jailed, shipwrecked, and finally lost his head, yet dared to proclaim, "Giving thanks always *for all things* unto God (Eph. 5:20, KJV, emphasis mine).

Celebrate your fortysomething days. Every last one of them. Don't you dare skip or low-key a single one of your birthdays.

Here are some suggestions for those readers who have never been called "party animals":

● *Change your image for the day.* Wear a new hairstyle, part it on the opposite side. If you normally wear dark colors, sample the rainbow. Or choose totally outrageous shoes to wear.

● *Dust off an activity that you have previously enjoyed but doesn't quite fit in with your normal routine or image.* Go blow bubbles in the park. Take friends to the zoo and feed the elephants! Rent the roller skating rink and have a birthday-skate!

● *Send yourself a card, cake, present, or a singing telegram.* Send it anonymously to the office. Remember to act surprised.[8]

● *Take the day off.*

● *Take a hike or fly a kite.*

● *Do something totally different that will leave your friends dumbfounded.* Book a hang gliding trip. Parachute out of a plane. Book a hot air balloon ride for you and your friends.

Sandra Burkhardt is a big believer in birthday celebrations. She suggests:

● *Go to a bookstore and buy yourself a coffee-table book.* Art, architecture, flower, or photography books will nourish your soul.

● *Plan an outrageous party.* Tell your friends "black tie," hire a bus, and take them to the circus or a professional wrestling match. Friends of mine in Phoenix rented a trolley car for a fortysomething, loaded forty of her friends, and toured the city announcing to everyone, "Marilyn is forty!"

● *If you have a summer birthday, do something cool.* Go skiing. If you have a winter birthday, have a beach party. Fill your living room with sand, heatlamps, and a small plastic pool.[9]

It's your birthday. Make something of it. And whatever you do, celebrate other fortysomething birthdays. This season called forty is a wonderful time to learn how to celebrate.

HOSPITALITY

Some of us don't know how to throw a good party. We act like we are kinfolks of the Prodigal Son's brother. Luke says he became angry and refused to attend his brothers "welcome home" salute. In fact, he got downright tacky and nasty: "Look! All these years I've been slaving for you and never disobeyed your orders. Yet you never gave me even a young goat so I could celebrate with my friends. But when this son of yours who has squandered your property with prostitutes comes home, you kill the fattened calf for him!" (Luke 15:29-30)

Paul, a single adult, certainly appreciated hospitality. Consider this juxtaposition of Scripture: "Practice hospitality" is preceded by "Share with God's people who are in need" (Rom. 12:13). While the text probably refers to physical need, there is room for it to apply to emotional need as well.

Single adults need to create moments, serendipities around a formica top kitchen table, picnic table, or a blanket spread under a tree.

We generally equate hospitality with formal entertaining but it encompasses much more — smiles, hugs, the whole range of human emotions.

Let's take a little test. Who has eaten at your dining table in the last month? Six months? Year? Name them. Who has munched popcorn by your fireplace, sipped iced tea on your deck, or lounged in your lawn chairs? Have you had overnight guests? Visiting nieces or nephews? College chums? Out-of-town guests?

Are you waiting to practice your hospitality until you buy a house? Or a *better* house? Or get new furniture? Or wallpaper the guestroom? *Or* until you have a spouse to cohost?

Most single adults have learned that people don't compare your accomodations to what they see in *Architectural Digest* or *House Beautiful.* In fact, some of those places look like a most unlikely place to have a party. I prefer those homes or apartments where the hosts put you at ease immediately by saying, "Overlook the mess and make yourself at home."

I admire those single adults who have that way of making a

kitchen, patio, or den "guest-friendly." Sitting around kitchen tables I have shared some of the most important issues of my heart.

What is the "warmest" place in your home or apartment? What can you do to "warm up" your abode? Candles, flowers, and small things can turn even tiny apartments into heart-warming places.

Try the following hospitality hints:

1. *Learn the gift of spontaneous hospitality.* I know single adults who "execute" hospitality. They manage 101 details and end up exhausted by the entire process. Everything has to be perfect or it's labeled a disaster. Such a mind-set does not constitute true hospitality.

2. *Invite.* Don't wait for someone else to invite you. And don't be upset if they don't reciprocate.

3. *Practice your hospitality skills on yourself.* Use a tablecloth, silver, cloth napkin, candle, flowers. Skip the paper plates and napkins. Put on your favorite music and enjoy, even if it's a TV dinner.

4. *Invite the Lord to join you and your guests.* Sanctify the event by seeking God's presence.

Profile of a Fortysomething: Kenneth Scott Latourette (1884–1968). Church historian, scholar, author of the classic seven volume *A History of the Expansion of Christianity*, and one-time president of the American Historical Society.

Dr. Latourette spent most of his academic career at Yale University. During his time, he organized fireside gatherings for students. "Usually," Latourette wrote in his biography, *Beyond the Ranges*, "I had not only a fire but apples." Students gathered by a fire in Latourette's rooms in Stuart Hall. Any student was welcomed, but Dr. Latourette expected regular attendance. Some years there was a core of theological conservatives, anxious for fellowship in an atmosphere they considered hostile to their faith traditions. Some participants had real doubts about their call to ministry or doctrines of the faith.

Many evenings, this scholarly bachelor sat back and let the students talk. Despite a heavy academic schedule, he gave priority to the groups and was almost never absent. On many occasions, Dr. Latourette served communion to that fellowship of students.

This scholar ate in the cafeteria, attended chapel and coffee hours, and made himself available to students. No few students called the learned scholar, "Uncle Ken." Students knew they could knock on his door and find a welcomed, "Come in."

Dr. Latourette wrote in his autobiography, "If, as an explorer, I have blazed trails into the 'never, never country,' of here and there—there have been lives who have seen, although dimly, His Son in me, that has been through no merit of mine, but because of His initiative God sent His whisper to me."

In the classroom, across a dining room, or by a crackling fire, this bachelor gave generous chunks of his time and helped shape hundreds of pastors and scholars. His faith shaped his hospitality.[10]

Look at Jesus' single friends: Mary, Martha, and Lazarus. Jesus loved to visit their home in Bethany. It was open to Him (John 12), although Luke reported one dinner party got off to a little rocky start. It seemed that Mary had parked herself at Jesus' feet, soaking up every word.

Martha, however, would have annoyed even Miss Manners. Luke said that she was "distracted by all the preparations that had to be made" (Luke 10:40). Imagine the leading bachelor in all Judea and the Crown Prince of heaven sitting in your living room and you can appreciate her anxiety. You can understand why Mary wasn't cooking in the kitchen.

Perhaps Martha had gotten tired of prodding Mary, "Oh Maryyyy . . . could you come here, *please!*" So she approached Jesus with an agenda.

"Lord, don't You care that my sister has left me to do the

work by myself?" [Can you hear the violins crescendoing in the background? I would love to have heard the tone of her next words.] "Tell her to help me!" (Luke 10:40)

Mary apparently isn't shamed by her sister's approach. Jesus says, "Martha. You are worried and upset about many things, but only one thing is needed. Mary has chosen what is better, and it will not be taken away from her" (Luke 10:41).

Real hospitality isn't "distracted by all the preparations." According to Dr. McAllaster, hospitality may be giving "someone your full attention, even if only for a few moments."[11]

As a forytsomething, learn to practice authentic hospitality. Remember, "If we are Christ's, then any guest we invite, ever, is also Christ himself. When we light candles and pour cups of hot wassail and ladle bowls of chili, we do it for Him. We do it in His name. Not in ours."[12]

CONCLUSION

Dragons face all of us. We can kill them, tame them, or drive them beyond the horizon. When the American pioneers conquered the western plains they found millions of wild horses. Did they say, "Oh no! Wild horses." Hardly, they tamed them and used them to turn the plains into farmland. I don't know exactly where one finds a harness and saddle for a dragon. But it can be done.

Fortysomething is an occasion to form some new habits and discard some old ones (like my overeating), to celebrate, to develop and practice the gifts of hospitality, and to replace some old tired memories.

Dr. Barnard was wrong. A single adult in his or her forties can still improve. By taking charge, it's never too late.

QUESTIONS

1. Can you think of ten ways to celebrate your life?
2. What habit do you need to eliminate?
3. What are the dragons you fear?
4. How would you like to celebrate your life?
5. Make a list of five people you can show hospitality to. Decide how, when, and where you can show hospitality.

Chapter Nine

THERE'S MORE
TO HAVING IT ALL
THAN HAVING IT ALL

*When I was as you are now, towering in the
confidence of twenty-one, little did I
suspect that I should be at forty-nine,
what I now am."*

— *Aristotle*

GOAL FOR FORTYSOMETHINGS: To make sense
of money.

Washington, D.C. was captivated by the young unmarried
woman from Montana. After working as a teacher in rural
schools, she had earned a graduate degree in social work and
had lobbied aggressively for women's right to vote.

Once Montana passed suffrage, Miss Jeannette Rankin announced her candidacy as a progressive Republican for Congress. And stunningly, in 1917, she was elected.

All the capital focused on the young "Congresslady," as she
was called — the first ever elected. President Wilson honored
her with a White House reception. She had it all: No woman
in American history had achieved so much.

April 6, 1917, four days after being sworn in, Miss Rankin
sat through the House debate on the proposed Declaration of
War against Germany. The media and seasoned politicians

speculated about how the rookie would vote.

On the roll call, after rancorous debate, she stood and said, through tears, "I want to stand by my country, but I cannot vote for war." The House was stunned—Jeannette Rankin had voted no; reporters scrambled for the phones. A majority had voted for war.

When the House adjourned, at 3 A.M. in the morning an exhausted Jeannette walked to her apartment, accompanied by her brother/adviser, who told her she had just "thrown away" everything she had worked so hard to gain, to say nothing of the damage to the political opportunities for other women.

"You won't be reelected!" he said with great emotion.

"I'm not interested in that. All I'm interested in is what they will say about me fifty years from now."

Women's groups who had honored her only days before now disowned her. Newspapers dismissed her as "silly and sentimental" and made much of the fact that she had been crying when she voted.

In 1918, just as her brother had predicted, Miss Rankin was defeated.[1]

The young single adult had had it all but she let it slip through her fingers. She could have had a long, comfortable career but she valued integrity more. Jeannette Rankin had learned one key lesson: There's more to having it all than having it all.

THE MYTH OF A LITTLE MORE

I am reminded me of a story about tycoon John D. Rockefeller.

"Sir," someone asked him, "how much money do you have?"

"A lot," the billionaire answered.

"Sir, how much money do you want?"

"A little bit more."

Headlines on the front pages for the last few years have focused on the indictments of major investment bankers and financial deal makers. Everything from fraud to insider trading has tarnished reputations and sent some financial geniuses to jail—they didn't pass go and they didn't collect $200 either. All of them were making outrageous salaries. So why did they break the law? Because they wanted "a little bit more."

Some fortysomethings—regardless of their incomes-always want "more." When I was growing up it was called keeping up with the Joneses. Today it is keeping up with the Trumps. Americans have an insatiable appetite for fast lane, jet-set lifestyles.

Webster defines *enough* as "occurring in such quantity, quality or scope as to fully satisfy demands or needs."

I thought I was beyond confronting greed until I paid the last car payment on my Honda—now three years old with only 28,000 miles on it. One afternoon as I walked, I passed a Honda dealership and found my eyes feasting on a new Accord. Quickly my eyes went to the sticker, and I didn't wince. Suddenly, I imagined myself driving that car!

While I could afford a new car I did not *need* a new car. So, I am still driving my red Honda. Reason prevailed, because thankfully I realized a new car would not fully satisfy my demands. Fortysomething is definitely a time to reassess one's financial situation.

JESUS ON GREED

One day a man interrupted Jesus, "Teacher, tell my brother to divide the inheritance with me" (Luke 12:13).

Jesus didn't ask the man to produce computer printouts of holdings, bank deposits, stock portfolios, or his certificates of deposit. Instead, He said, "Man, who appointed Me a judge or arbiter between you?" [That, however, wasn't the end of the story.] Jesus added, "Watch out! Be on your guard against all kinds of greed; a man's life does not consist in the abundance of his possessions" (Luke 12:14-15).

Jesus slipped in a "gotcha" phrase: "all kinds of greed." What kind of things would Jesus include in greed: Money? Power? Status/prestige? A beautiful body? Happiness? Fame? Success? A best-seller?

Would Jesus exclude marriage? Or a sex life? Or a family

with 2.3 kids, the dog, and a white picket fence? Remember, Moses cautioned us against coveting *anything* that belongs to our neighbor.

Jesus had their attention — and it's no coincidence that E.F. Hutton's ads have been so effective: "When E.F. Hutton talks, people listen" — money gets people's attention. Let's examine a story Jesus told. And let's assume the main character in this story was a single adult, perhaps fortysomething.

⌐The ground of a certain rich man produced a good crop. He thought to himself, "What shall I do? I have no place to store my crops."

Then he said, "This is what I'll do. I will tear down my barns and build bigger ones, and there I will store all my grain and my goods. And I'll say to myself, 'You have plenty of good things laid up for many years. Take life easy; eat, drink and be merry' " (Luke 12:16-19).

Now, if this guy were around today, no doubt, he would have his own cable talk show, a best-seller with his picture on the cover, and maybe even be doing an American Express commercial. He'd be on committees, boards, and letterheads and would never get a bad table at a good restaurant. However, Jesus finished the story with a sobering ending:

"But God said to him, 'You fool! This very night your life will be demanded from you. Then who will get what you have prepared for yourself?' " (Luke 12:20)

It's one thing to be called a fool by some angry driver at a stoplight. It is another thing to have God call you a fool. Jesus must have sensed His audience gloating over the fate of a "certain rich man." He spoiled their glee.

"This is how it will be with anyone who stores things up for himself but is not rich toward God" (Luke 12:21). Jesus' "anyone" includes you and me.

WHAT IS GREED?
Webster defines *greed* as "excessive or reprehensible acquisitiveness." Quickly it is a question of perspective. How much

is too much to pay for a hamburger? If you are a minimum wage earner, $5.95 for a burger is a lot. If you are a Wall Street lawyer, it would be only pocket change.

We are early conditioned not to covet. We are early conditioned to "be nice and share." But two words merit a closer look: envy and greed. Envy is my wanting what *you* have. Greed is my wanting *more* of what I have.

Lawrence Shames in his book, *The Hunger For More: Searching for Values in an Age of Greed*, insists that a craving for more is in "the national bloodstream." "The habit of more has been installed as the operative truth among the economically ambitious."[2]

In 1990, American's unpaid credit loans totaled $795 billion (up from $300 billion in 1980). Moreover, the combined unpaid balance on credit cards has risen to $2,042 per card holder (in 1980 the average card owner owed only $931 outstanding on his or her credit cards). Not all of this can be attributed to the effects of inflation.[3]

WHAT'S WRONG WITH A LITTLE GREED?

Americans love the "How I made my billions" books that periodically appear on the best-seller lists. Where else but in America? Go back to Jesus' story and count all the I's and mes and mines. This story is packed with personal pronouns.

I saw this T-shirt in Washington: "No Condo. No MBA. No BMW." All America has seen the bumper sticker: "The One With the Most Toys Wins!" No wonder the book, *How to Have More in a Have Not World* was must reading to get ahead.[4]

Joe Barnhart complains of what he calls "The Christian Yuppie Club" composed "of narcissistic self-indulgers, people who imagine that they have earned all their good fortune and that those at the bottom of the heap deserve to be there either because God did not see fit to endow them with comparable talents or because they have not tried to help themselves."[5]

In this day, too often, the evangelical answer to America's growing hungry and homeless is "Get a job! Read a power of

positive thinking classic!" If we take this attitude, we will
have trouble with John's words, "We ought to lay down our
lives for our brothers. If anyone has material possessions and
sees his brother in need but has not pity on him, how can the
love of God be in him?" (1 John 3:16-17)

HOW DO I KNOW IF I AM UNDER THE INFLUENCE?

Driving under the influence of alcohol is a serious offense in
most states. When stopped, drivers will argue "I'm not
drunk." While some are not legally drunk, they are certainly
under alcohol's influence.

Much the same is true of greed. Some fortysomethings—
like an alcoholic in denial—argue, "I can handle my greed."

Simply, the question is greed by whose standards? For example, during all the ruckus over the lifestyle of certain TV
evangelists, I kept thinking of the late Joe Bayly's observation
that to the poor Chinese peasant or the starving African, even
a new, shiny, stripped-down Honda looks luxurious.

Many fortysomethings have difficulty appreciating their
comparative good fortune. We compare ourselves to other
Americans rather than to the citizens of the world. The poor-
est American would be quite wealthy by Third-world
standards.

Profile of a Fortysomething: Charles Simeon
(1759–1836). Ordained in the Church of England in
1783. For fifty-three years Simeon pastored the Church
of the Holy Trinity in Cambridge and became the light-
ening rod for the evangelical movement in England.

Simeon offered three criteria by which one could know
if he/she were under the influence of greed: (1) the
manner in which we seek the "treasures," (2) the manner in which we enjoy the treasures, and (3) the manner
in which we mourn the loss of our treasures.

Once in preaching on the text, "Will a man rob God?"
(Mal. 3:8) he let his words reverberate through the

church: "*You* have all robbed Him!" Then pointing his finger in various directions said, "You! and You! and You!"

Charles Simeon lived a frugal life that qualified him to preach on the theme so earnestly. Pastor Simeon used much of his money to help pastors in small churches.

Simeon wrote on the fiftieth anniversary as pastor: "I can appeal to all who have ever known me, that to proclaim a suffering and triumphant Messiah, as revealed to us by Moses and the prophets, has been the one object of my life, without any variation . . . without ever turning aside after novelties, or fond conceits or matters of doubtful disputation."[6]

Simeon's exhortation is challenging. Will that be said of you when you are seventy-two? Jesus gave two powerful injunctions: "Watch out" and "Be on your guard against all kinds of greed." Periodically, we should analyze our financial habits accordingly.

WHAT ARE THE CONSEQUENCES OF GREED?
The love of money has tragic consequences. Let's examine them.

• *Things rich/people poor.* One of the most evident proofs that money won't buy happiness is the life of Howard Hughes. Although one of the nation's most brilliant and wealthiest men, he never had a lasting relationship and died a frightened old man. Alone, he was money rich, but people poor.

• *Poor criteria of success.* Ask many single adults what is success and most answers will be $$$. Scully Blotnick addressed this in his book, *Ambitious Men: Their Drives, Dreams, and Delusions* and identified four key elements: (1) fortune, (2) fame, (3) power, and (4) prestige. With the first you can buy the next three.[7]

Yet, across the centuries Jesus' question deserves an answer: "What good is it for a man to gain the whole world, yet forfeit his soul? Or what can a man give in exchange for his soul?" (Mark 8:36-37)

• *Coasting.* How much money is enough? That's still *the* question to be asked. Charles Hayden, in 1886, after a year's apprenticeship as a mining stock broker, borrowed $20,000 and set up the firm of Hayden, Stone, and Company. Even after he had a seat on the New York Stock Exchange, Charles still counted pennies. Once he hesitated buying a list of potential investors for a mere $25.

Finally he splurged and bought the list; that decision led to a spectacular financial windfall and a very secure financial future for the young bachelor. Charles Hayden's role model must have been Ebenezer Scrooge, also unmarried. Hayden hated unproductive moments, distractions, and lazy workers. Visitors were given only a few moments of his "valuable" time; he often held board and committee meetings simultaneously to save time.

When asked why he had remained a bachelor he explained, "I married the firm of Hayden, Stone, and Company, and you are all my big family."[8]

Charles Hayden's commitment to making a dollar would make him a patron saint to many Americans today.

WHAT WILL I DO ABOUT MY GREED?

You can do something about your greed. Try the following. *Decision 1: Evaluate your greed.* It's so difficult to sing that black spiritual and think about greed at the same time:

Not my brother, not my sister
But it's me O Lord
Standing in the need of prayer.

In this case standing in the need of confrontation. Have you honestly confronted greed, first person singular? Would you be comfortable letting someone examine your checkbook to look at your spending patterns?

Here are some good questions to help you evaluate your greed:

(1) Is my greed making my life unhappy?

(2) Is my "mild-mannered" greed affecting my spiritual, or physical growth?

(3) Does my greed/need cause me to think less of myself?

(4) Does my greed/need distract me from my work, relationships, or church involvement?

(5) Do I justify my greed/need by telling myself that I deserve it because I work so hard?

(6) Does my greed/need keep me from giving as generously to the church or charities as I wish?

(7) Has my greed/need created an embarrassing credit or debt problem?

These questions make me uncomfortable. Still they need to be asked, every payday.

Decision 2: Determine your need. There is a proverb that suggests if your outgo exceeds your income, your upkeep will lead to your downfall! Fortysomethings can testify to the validity of that wisdom.

I am learning that five simple words can increase my savings and cut down on debt: *Do I really need this?*

When a local single adult group in Kansas City had a garage sale to earn some money for a missions trip, they asked if I would care to contribute anything. I contributed a truckload of "stuff"—I hasten to add not junk. They were things I had grown weary of, that no longer suited me. As I filled the truck I kept asking, "What possessed me to buy this in the first place?"

Perhaps my questioning was triggered by something I learned in a financial seminar. For every dollar you invest at age twenty-five you will earn $17 by retirement.[9] If only I had put that money in a bank account instead of buying all those electronic gadgets and gourmet hamburgers.

Belle Bennett, gave her life as a single adult to building women's ministries in the Methodist Episcopal Church, South—forerunner of today's United Methodist Church. Belle devoted countless hours to raising money to launch Scarritt College for training missionaries and Christian educators.

Such a training center cost a great deal of money, even in

the 1890s and many males feared theological training for women, saying, "They might take over the church!"

Even though Belle had grown up in wealth, once she poured her life into this cause, she lived in a small hotel room in Richmond, Kentucky. During her travels, she locked her valuables in a closet, so that her room could be rented in her absence. That money paid for college educations for several women. Moreover, during all her years of service to the Methodist Church she never received a salary, and often not even expense money. How did she survive financially? Belle Bennett knew how to distinguish her needs from her wants.[10]

Here are some helpful hints to consider for abstaining from obtaining:

- *Resist* the ads and commercials. Just because it is advertised on TV, doesn't mean that you have to buy it.
- *Relinquish* your clout. OK, you've got a wallet full of plastic. Keep it in there.
- *Rehearse* your nos and "NOs!"
- *Reorder* your priorities. What do you want to do with your money?

Decision 3: Invest your seed. God wants you to be a conduit. I am not endorsing anything that smacks of "giving to get." But God blesses you so that you can contribute to the needs of the kingdom. Paul said, "See that you also excel in this grace of giving" (2 Cor. 8:7) and later in the same chapter added, "your plenty will supply what they need" (v. 14).

Many fortysomethings would take Paul to task: "Wait, you haven't seen my checkbook." I don't think that would have moved Paul to reconsider; I suspect he lived with a zero balance in funds. He wrote to Titus, "Do everything you can to help Zenas the lawyer and Apollos on their way and see that they have everything they need (Titus 3:13). Paul was saying: Invest in their ministry.

Today there are a lot of ministries that aren't getting what they need, and sometimes because they haven't learned the sophisticated giving schemes and tactics that work so well on evangelicals. And sometimes because some of us have short pockets due to our credit card addiction. What can you do?

YOU CAN CHANGE

Recommit your stewardship. Determine what kind of steward you want to be: minimal or generous? If stewardship isn't part of your financial priorities by the time the bills are paid there won't be much left. And if you don't set it aside for giving, it will become your *Oh-no!* fund used to bail you out of the emergencies.

In writing about Belle Bennett I was moved by her stewardship because I graduated from the college she founded. If she had been stingy, I would have earned my M.A. somewhere else. One biographer noted, "Like Mary of old, she broke the precious ointment of a wonderfully fragrant life, and poured it out, gladly, instinctively, at her Lord's feet."[11] Will that be said about me?

On more than one occasion family friends questioned this single woman's giving. One said, "To give was the first requisite of her nature."[12] Many shook their heads at her reckless generosity and predicted she would end up poor and destitute.

Paul declared, "Whoever sows sparingly will also reap sparingly, and whoever sows generously will also reap generously" (2 Cor. 9:6). I realize this is a popular verse with the "give-to-get" crowd. But it preceeds, "Each [single] should give what he [she] has decided in his [her] heart to give, not reluctantly or under compulsion, for God loves a cheerful giver" (v. 7).

It's so easy to talk about sacrificial giving and to hum "I Surrender All" while walking through the electronic gadgetry of our apartments, condos, and houses. But do we have to have CD players, tape decks, TVs, Walkmans, personal computers, and so many this and thats?

Save. Making savings a regular on-going part of cashing your paychecks. Initially, because of debt, you may not be able to put away much. But start with something for every forty-something payday.

Wear it out. Fortysomethings are hooked on the *newest* and

latest and *biggest* and *best* and *improved*, the buzz words of
fortysomethings. One person looked at my stereo system and
snarled, "Thieves would never want that! Matter-of-fact, they
might even take pity on you and bring you something better."

There's nothing wrong with wearing out a product or item
before replacing it (although putting aside some money to
replace it as it wears out is practical thinking).

Release it's grip. Sometimes it is difficult for fortysomethings
to know if we possess something or if it possesses us.
Remember Charles Simeon's criteria about greed: *how we
mourn something's loss.*

The Bible speaks to this issue. "For everything in the
world—the cravings of sinful man, the lust of his eyes and the
boasting of what he has and does—comes not from the Father
but from the world. The world and its desires pass away, but
the man [single] who does the will of God lives forever"
(1 John 2:16-17).

CONCLUSION

These days single adults have to make sense of their money.
It's easy in a day of leveraged buy outs and hostile takeovers
to let the world squeeze us into its consumer mold. But
there's more to having it all than having it all. Scrooge learned
that one Christmas night and some adults will learn that during their fortysomething pilgrimage.

I recently heard the story of a man who gave "all" he had to
God—about $20—in an offering. He became a millionaire. He
toured the United States giving his testimony of "having giv-
en his all to God." At the conclusion of one of the services, a
woman walked up and asked, "Would you be willing to give it
all, *again?*"

Integrity does count. Today, tourists visiting the U.S. Capitol, will pass a larger-than-life bronze of Jeannette Rankin,
dedicated sixty-eight years after she counted the cost, bucked
the tide of public opinion, and said, "No."[12]

You too can make a difference. You can commit your time
and energy and money to institutions and causes that will live
long after you are gone.

QUESTIONS

1. In what ways do greed and envy influence you? Your spending? Your saving? Your giving?
2. Are you accountable to anyone for your financial habits? If not, who might you ask to assist you?
3. Name three people you would allow to look through your checkbook/canceled checks. What would they find out about your lifestyle?
4. Are you a giver? Which of the following adjectives best describes your giving—generous, stingy, dutifully, joyfully?
5. Are you a saver? What specific things should you be saving for as a matter of financial principle?

Chapter Ten

HEROES IN AN AGE OF CELEBRITIES

So little done, so much to do.
—dying words of Cecil Rhodes

GOAL FOR FORTYSOMETHINGS: To reexamine our heroes.

Andy Warhol may be as remembered for one quote as for his art. Warhol once prophesied of a world where "Everyone will be famous for fifteen minutes."[1]

Anne M. Gorsuch, former Administrator of the Environmental Protection Agency, was shopping in a market one day after her well-publicized firing. A shopper noticed her and followed her. As they passed the zucchini, the woman demanded, "Excuse me, didn't you *used* to be somebody?"[2]

Today, "getting there" is not enough — you have to hold on. All around there is a hunger to debunk, to demyth, to dethrone. Not just to tarnish the halo but to zap it into a million pieces. In a world where everybody is famous for fifteen minutes why should one person hog the spotlight?

In such a world we have a big appetite for "lite" heroes.

Disposable celebrities have become a symbolic fast food and Americans are desperate for replacements.

Once upon a time, Americans believed in heroes: Presidents, military figures, business tycoons, and athletes. Innocence prevailed in the mind of the American public concerning those giants. We honored them because we respected them and their office or achievements.

But times have changed. During the last decade, most fortysomethings have witnessed a debacle in Southeast Asia, the resignation of a President to avoid impeachment, the bargained settlement that led to the ouster of the Speaker of the House, the Iran-Contra scandal, and a Supreme Court nominee who smoked pot as a professor at Harvard. To say the least, there has been an enormous erosion of confidence in public figures. "They're all the same!" some fortysomethings snarl. This attitude impacts voter apathy.

While the shenanigans are not new, these days a highly sophisticated news media—celebrities themselves—seems determined to sift through every detail. This means rummaging through trash cans, emotionally and literally, for tidbits to offer on the evening news.

Against such a reality, how does a fortysomething read the "Hall of Fame" passage in Hebrews 11 about "giants" who "through faith conquered kingdoms, administered justice, and gained what was promised; who shut the mouths of lions, quenched the fury of the flames, and escaped the edge of the sword; whose weakness was turned to strength; and who became powerful in battle and routed foreign enemies. Woman received back their dead, raised to life again. Others were tortured and refused to be released, so that they might gain a better resurrection. Some faced jeers and flogging, while still others were chained and put in prison, put to death by the sword. They went about in sheepskins and goatskins, destitute, persecuted, and mistreated" (Heb. 11:33-37).

In 1990, I again visited Debrovnik, Yugoslavia and the Franciscan monastery of the Little Brothers. That monastery since 1590, through a succession of monks, has been writing what they call(ed) the *martyrologum* or short biographies of the saints to encourage today's saints-to-be.

But evangelicals don't want martyrs. We want a Christian Miss America, or a Christian U.S. Senator. We want Christian professional athletes and business tycoons.

The classic hymn "The Church's One Foundation" describes a "mystic sweet communion with those whose rest is won." But how do we have "mystic sweet communion" in an age of the fifteen-minute hero? Rabbi Joshua Herschel comments on our culture, "Poets applaud the absurd, novelists explore the decadent, and men prostrate themselves before the deities of lust and power. Our [national] obsession is with human flesh. . . . Daily we are bombarded by lurid reports of the mass killer, the rapist, and the corrupt bureaucrat. The fantasies of even little children are now peopled with perverts and the radiated dead."[3] The Rabbi follows with a chilling question: "Who will speak of those who did justice, loved mercy, and walked humbly?"[4]

Fortysomethings must ask, "Who are my heroes?" As Christian fortysomethings living in the age of the celebrity, the media giant, and the kiss-and-tell biography, do we appreciate those who do justice, love mercy, and walk humbly before the Lord? Or in the age of the "no deposit/no return" are we passively letting our culture mass market the latest batch of "lite" heroes whose only claim to fame is the size of their bosom or bank account, or the amount of their latest "deal" or the number of points scored in a game?

In the Age of Celebrities, we easily forget the quiet heroes and heroines who live without pomp, fanfare, or exposure on the six o'clock news. We have a place in our society for a token Mother Teresa or two. But most singles see no link whatsoever between her example and our everyday lives.

THE EPIDEMIC OF CYNICISM

In an age when U.S. presidents creatively tell the truth or selectively remember the truth such as one President who told Congress and grand juries "I don't remember" but then signed a $5 million contract to write his memoirs, why are we surprised by cynicism? It is a time when "the truth, the whole truth and nothing but the truth" is a standard only in some courtrooms. When athletes fail drug tests, no wonder we cover our eyes in despair. Still most of us peek through our fingers for the first glimpse of the next hero or celebrity.

Cynicism may be developing into our national pastime. Like bowling pins: set 'em up and watch 'em fall. Our heroes don't last. Everything's plastic these days, including heroes.

AN ACHE FOR SPECIALNESS

One of the by-products of the abortion debate is a refueling of the psalmist's question, "What is man that Thou art mindful of him?" (Ps. 8:4, RSV) There is a basic human desire to feel we count—that our lives have meaning. We don't want to believe we were a biological accident—a by-product of an amorous rendezvous.

Daniel Taylor addressed this in an insightful article, "The Fear of Insignificance." Taylor described strolling through the beautiful Prince's Street Gardens in Edinburgh, and finding a churchyard cemetery. That day, a flea market was being held in the cemetery with second-hand clothes hung on a line between one tombstone and the next. That resurrected in him a fear, common among many fortysomethings: the fear of having lived an *insignificant* life. Taylor wrote: "Will it matter, once I am gone, that I was ever here? And yet who in the flea market crowd sorting among the leftovers of contemporary lives, had ever had a passing thought for [the] prestige, wealth, and power of those buried there?"[5]

There is a haunting question that I cannot shake these days: Who will remember me one hundred years from now?

Fortysomethings have an innate ache for specialness in a time when celebrity worship may be becoming a secular religion. All of us need heroes: genuine, bona fide, bigger than life, card-carrying heroes and heroines.

WHAT MAKES A HERO?

1. *A hero sees opportunities where others see troubles.* Tiananmen Square, Peking, June 1989. As Army tanks rolled toward the

demonstrators for democracy, one courageous single adult walked out in front of eighteen army tanks.

The tanks stopped. For three minutes the world basked in a hero's presence. This young Chinese man saw an opportunity and spontaneously seized it.

2. *The hero must do something that makes a difference.* The hero knows *where* to start and *when* to act: Kipling wrote, "If you can keep your head when all about you are losing theirs. . . ." Heroes can.

Profile of a Fortysomething: Joseph de Vuester (1840–1889). Humanitarian and advocate. When leprosy was first discovered in Hawaii in 1853, the public hysteria decreed that lepers be abandoned on an obscure island named Molokai. All lepers were required by law to report to authorities within fourteen days of diagnosis for banishment to Molokai. The colony quickly became hell on earth. *Aolo kanawai ma keia wahi:* In this place there is no law. Orgies, drunkenness, nakedness, and debauchery were routine. The strong preyed on the weak.

Once Joseph de Vuester learned of the living conditions on Molokai he decided to do something about them. With his bishop's permission, he went to the island to establish a church and hospital. The islanders who greeted him when he stepped onto the beach, "seemed to be but remnants of human beings, rotted and bloated beyond ordinary shape."[6]

Joseph hardly knew where to begin to restore sanity and order. But once he discovered that packs of wild dogs invaded the fresh graves, he set to building strong fences to keep out the dogs.

De Vuester realized if he were to minister to the lepers — to win their confidence — he could show no hint of fear of contracting leprosy or repulsion at their bodies. So, he chose to eat with them, even to share their utensils and dishes.

De Vuester went to work to lobby for his lepers. Many

ships would not even dock to unload supplies for the colony. When de Vuester requested fresh meat, cows were shipped but were pushed into the sea some distance from shore. Some captains did the same with lepers.

In desperation, de Vuester (or Father Damien as he became known) left the colony to personally appeal to the Board of Public Health in Honolulu. Officials responded rudely to this kindhearted single adult. When de Vuester presented his "want list" for supplies and medicine, he was told to concern himself with the leper's spiritual needs. He was soon branded a troublemaker and warned that he would be arrested if he ever left the colony again.

De Vuester returned to his life of building coffins, small houses, a church, and a school. Daily he personally washed and bandaged the wounds of many lepers. Slowly dignity was restored to the island. De Vuester organized bands and orchestras, picnics and festivals.

Initially, he referred to himself as a leper, figuratively. "As for me, I make myself a leper, to gain all to Jesus." In June 1885, however, the forty-five-year-old startled his congregation by opening his sermon with "*We lepers*" instead of his usual, "My brethren." De Vuester had contracted leprosy. When others would have given up, he responded, "Rest? It is no time to rest now, when there is so much left to do and my time is so short."[7]

Still he battled with the bureaucracy in Honolulu until Robert Louis Stevenson — one of the world's leading writers — visited the colony and wrote glowingly about de Vuester's work. Suddenly the world took notice.

A short time later, the Queen, Liliuokalani visited the colony. What was scheduled for a one hour visit turned into an all-day affair. She told de Vuester that she found it hard to believe he could stay in such a place.

"It is my work," he explained. "You see, Madame, they are my parishioners."[8] The Queen's eyes filled with tears.

At the end of the day, as she prepared to board her ship, the Queen offered her hand to Damien. The crowd gasped. A queen offering her hand to a leper? After Damien bent low and kissed her hand, she wept like a heartbroken child.

Once aboard ship, she spoke to no one until she reached Honolulu. Reporters raced off the ship to file their stories and suddenly the Board of Health was besieged with calls for action. The eyes of the world turned to de Vuester on Molokai.

The queen never forgot the leper priest/humanitarian. She wrote, "I know well that your labors and sacrifices have no other motives than the desire to do good to those in distress; and that you look for no reward but from the great God, our sovereign Lord, who directs and inspires you."[9]

She decorated him to the Royal Order of Kalakukuy. De Vuester modestly put the decoration into a box. Decorations, he noted, were for heroes, and he was but a middle-aged priest with a lot of work to do. Yet, he treasured the Queen's signature on the letter signed "your friend."

Father Damien, as he was now called, died at age forty-eight on Good Friday, noting, "the good Lord is calling me to keep Easter with Himself."[10]

One man changed the world's attitudes toward lepers.

3. *The hero will not accommodate his/her vision to contemporary social or cultural values.* A hero doesn't offer excuses. As a forty-eight-year-old bachelor, Grover Cleveland had easily won the Democratic party's nomination for President in 1884. After all, he had been the reform mayor of Buffalo, then Governor of New York. The Republicans had denied the nomination to President Chester Arthur and had turned to a political favorite named James G. Blaine. Because there were few real issues, the campaign soured into name-calling quickly. The Democrats had charged that Blaine had been guilty of unethical

conduct in his involvement with the railroads.

The Republicans retaliated by charging that Cleveland had fathered an illegitimate son. The Democrats, frightened of seeing their chances for the White House whither on the vine, pleaded with Cleveland to deny the charges.

Governor Cleveland—who *had* fathered the boy and *had* always supported the child and his mother, Maria Halpin, answered in three words: "Tell the truth."

Today party leaders and aides would want to assess "damage control." His spokesman would stonewall it and issue an outraged denial. Instead, this single adult admitted his fault and was elected by about 23,000 votes. At the age of forty-eight Grover Cleveland became the first Democratic president since the Civil War and his unmarried sister became the "First Lady."[11] There's a lesson for today's fortysomethings: Tell the truth.

4. *The hero points single adults to new possibilities of what we might be and do.* How can fortysomethings evaluate heroes in an age of celebrities? Here are some suggestions that work for me.

• *Read more biography.* How many solid biographies have you read in the last year? Are you familiar with the biographical reference works in your local library? You can start with *The Dictionary of American Biography* (18,000 entries). The next time you are bored, try skimming one of the volumes. You'll come away with some fresh heroes.

I also recommend *The International Dictionary of Twentieth Century Biography* by Edward Vernoff and Rima Shore. (New American Library, 1987). This contains more than 5,600 short biographies of leading figures from around the world: politics, literature, the arts, the sciences, and popular culture. It's a great coffee table book for casual reading.

You need to "stock" your mind with good biographical material. Read for your future as well. Christian biographies will inspire fortysomethings to redouble their efforts to emulate the great "cloud of witnesses" who urge us to "throw off everything that hinders" and to "run with perseverance the race marked out for us" (Heb. 12:1).

● *Do thorough research on your heroes.* Hero hunting can be a part of your annual vacation or a mini trip. For example I have long been impressed with Angelina and Sarah Grimke — leaders in the anti-slavery movement and the first women to speak in public in America. So, when I found myself in Boston, I went to the State House in Boston to see where these two single adults made history; when in Charleston, South Carolina I visited their home.

In Tennessee I researched Harry T. Burn. This single adult debunked the notion that one man cannot make a difference. Harry T. Burn changed his vote on a roll call vote in 1920 in the Tennessee legislature. So what?

He voted "Yes!" on the ratification of the Nineteenth Amendment to give women the right to vote in all federal elections. The amendment passed by one vote: Harry's. Tennessee was the last legislature to ratify the Amendment.

I went to the gallery of the House of Representatives where Christians waved their Bibles and yelled that God didn't want women voting: The idea that a black woman's vote equaled a white man's offended God. As I sat there, I tried to imagine the pressure on that twenty-five-year-old. The Christians had threatened to defeat anyone in the next election who didn't vote their way.

I walked down the stairwell he walked down in the old Union Station in Nashville to board a train to go home and explain to his constituents in McMinn County why he voted against their wishes.

Harry was not reelected. But he is a hero.[12]

● *Remember that biographical reading is a way of obeying the scriptural injunction to "remember."* The Jews were reminded to "remember what the Lord had done." Through biography we remember the courage of giants and find inspiration for our own.

● *Praise the common man.* Read biographic material for the qualities that can transfer from the hero to your life.

In 1980, an unknown electrician worked hard to support his wife and six children, trying to make ends meet. Called a "delinquent worshiper" he and faith had had a parting of the ways, that is, until life grew harder. The electrician explained, "I was incapable of saying anything in public. My tongue used to outrun my mind. I was unable to keep track of the words I said. I would always speak before I thought and was therefore a poor public speaker. Come August, things changed. I don't know how it happened. The agnostics would probably interpret it as necessity, as something I was forced to do by the flow of events. . . . Something occurred, which I do not comprehend. . ."[13]

Within twelve months, he had organized a union, led a strike at Gdansk, a Baltic seaport, and was the topic of conversation from Moscow to Washington, D.C. Within that same year he had a Nobel Peace Prize, his face on the cover of *Time* as Man of the Year, and a permanent police escort and record of harassment.

Lech Walesa, a common man has systematically humiliated the Communist government of Poland. "I simply believe in providence," he has said. "That is precisely why I can accomplish significantly more than if I were just Lech Walesa, without God directing my fate. It's good to have the awareness of that great force outside us and above us directing our lives."[14]

Who will be the next Lech Walesa? Perhaps you. Motivational speakers say to us: "Make a difference." But generally, under our breaths we say, "Who me?" Why not you?

● *Incorporate more biography into your thinking.* Biographical material is not merely an alternative to television. It is a basic ingredient in balanced thinking and decision-making.

Phillip Berman incorporated personal experience and biography in a wonderful book, *The Courage of Conviction.* In 1974, as he watched his father die with cancer, Berman confronted three questions:

(1) Who am I?
(2) Why am I here?
(3) Where did I come from and where am I going?

Every fortysomething has to face those questions. Berman, as he wrestled with them, came to a simple conclusion: "I believe that we live in a time when a number of people are hungry for meaning but have not the courage to seek it."[15]

So, he decided to write a book on courage. Instead of filling it with quotations and insights from philosophers, sociologists, and psychologists, Berman wrote a number of notables and asked them to talk about courage in their lives. Billy Graham, Norman Cousins, Hugh Downs, Lech Walesa, Madeline L'Engle, and forty others responded with fascinating biographic essays that have been a source of encouragement to me.

• *Make a difference.* Fortysomethings must make a difference by embracing solid heroes rather than the instant heroes our culture promotes.

We make a difference by holding up heroes — real, godly difference-makers, to children, young adults, and other single adults. We can say through our biographic reading and admiration, this was a person whose obedience brought a smile to the face of God.

A single adult, Katherine Lee Bates, wrote "America the Beautiful" and included these important words:

O beautiful for heroes proved
In liberating strife,
Who more than self their country loved
And mercy more than life!
America! America! May God thy gold refine
Till all success be nobleness
And every gain divine.

Are we willing to declare that real success is in fact — not just in sentiment — nobleness and righteousness?

• *Fortysomethings must cautiously consider their role in hero-bashing.* Hero bashing, once started, is difficult to stop.

At the risk of alienating some readers, let me identify my hero. In 1980, he looked like a bearded Old Testament prophet, rather than one of the nations' leading pediatric surgeons. When President Reagan nominated him for Surgeon General, evangelicals were enthusiastic because of his antiabortion stand; liberals and feminists were hysterical. His confirmation by the Senate was delayed for a year.

Eight years passed. One of the greatest epidemics in the

history of humankind has this nation in a death grip, and one man stepped forward to guide the nation's medical response. Is it mere coincidence that he is a dedicated believer?

The people who had initially cheered turned on the good doctor from Philadelphia and became like dogs biting at his heels. Christians picketed his testimonial dinner; Republican politicians rechecked their date books and sent regrets. One conservative said, "He should have kept his lip buttoned."[16]

Many evangelicals could associate only one word with Dr. C. Everett Koop: condoms. He had "peddled" condoms, they charged, ignoring the fact that every statement Koop made on condoms was preceded with a qualifier on abstinence. Too many heard only what they wanted to hear.

We did not come to his defense. He left office, betrayed by many Christians. Still he may well come to be recognized, by social and medical historians, as *the* most outstanding Surgeon General in the history of the Republic.

I've tried to make sense of him. What has made him so compassionate toward AIDS patients — those the evangelical community has rejected. Dr. Koop repeatedly said, "I'm not the nation's chaplain general. I'm the surgeon general of all the people."[17]

Why is Koop a hero to millions? Because he stuck to his principles. Observers note, "Just as his deep religious belief in the sacredness of human life had impelled him to become one of the most zealous leaders of the antiabortion movement and had driven him to champion Baby Doe, so his deep faith now [motivated] Koop to stand up for those whose lives were menaced by AIDS. Every life deserved protection, believed Koop, even those he felt had been badly led. No one was to be left behind. He would never give in to the forces of social/medical triage."[18]

But is C. Everett Koop a bona fide, card-carrying hero or a well-placed celebrity?

Ask the doctor. "I think that people will look back and say," Koop admitted to one researcher, " 'he was a lone voice crying in the wilderness. He rose to a position of notoriety because in an era when there weren't many heroes around, he *appeared* to be one.' ''[19]

What has made this man so compassionate? Koop's compassion is born of personal pain. In 1968, his single adult son, David, was killed in a mountain climbing accident. Thousands of parents know that Dr. Koop is not some government bureaucrat, fat cat, or highrolling country club doctor. He is a parent who has lost a son. His heart has been broken.

CONCLUSION

So, this decade is definitely the right time to reexamine our heroes. This decade is a time to read more biography. It's time to do thorough research on our heroes. It's time to remember the common, courageous man—like the Chinese pro-democracy demonstrator who on June 5, 1989, as Army tanks advanced on Tiananmen Square, dared to step in front of them. Much to the surprise of the world—the tanks stopped. And a lot of fortysomethings shook our heads in disbelief at such courage. What a hero!

On some distant day, we will hear the Lord announce His "Hall of Fame." I suspect some real surprises. We may spend the first 100 years saying, "Never heard of 'em."

The Lord's standards of success and achievement are not necessarily synonymous with that of twentieth-century American evangelicals.

Can my "saints" and heroes compete with the continuous parade of celebrities by our culture? Those who have "it all" according to the standards of most fortysomethings?

Do I respect those precious few people who love justice, who do mercy, and who walk humbly with the Lord?

QUESTIONS

1. Make a list of your heroes. Why are they heroes to you?
2. Who were your heroes as a child, as a teen, and as a young adult?
3. How do celebrities influence your life?
4. Review your list of heroes. Which of them do justice, love mercy, and walk humbly with the Lord?
5. Will it matter, once you are gone, that you lived? How so?

Chapter Eleven

WHERE WILL YOU BE WHEN YOU GET TO WHERE YOU'RE GOING?

> *But have no fear—here come the baby boomers to lay waste to another assumption. Forty isn't over the hill, it's prime! Who says so? We say so—and there are more of us than there are of anybody else, so the message gets out loud and clear.*
>
> *—Lee Eisenberg*

GOAL FOR FORTYSOMETHINGS: To befriend the season.

I seldom read Oil of Olay ads, but this one caught my eye. The two page white-on-black ad consisted of these words: "I don't intend to grow old gracefully ... I intend to fight it every step of the way." Well, I agree with that philosophy.

We've come a long way since chapter one but I am still taken by Sue Bender's haunting question, "Is there another way to lead a good life?"[1] I hope that after reading *Fortysomething and Single* and out of your own experience and pilgrimage you can say yes. Simply, as Paul Tournier discovered, "What matters is not our experiences but the fact that *in them* we have known the power of God's grace."[2]

There are no super-savers or discounts through this season for committed single adults. Let's review the choices that can help us answer affirmatively.

CHOICE 1: Admit That You Are Forty

Forty is not such a bad age. Moses killed the Egyptian at forty and fled to Midian, where he spent the next forty years as a shepherd (Acts 7:23-30). Jacob received his blessing at age forty. Joshua was forty when Moses sent him to explore the Promised Land.

The Lord's words to Joshua, "There is much land yet to be conquered" (Josh. 13:1, my paraphrase) could have appeared in every chapter of this book. The forties are a land to be explored, conquered, and ultimately harvested.

His name was Hoshea, son of Nun and he was a leader of the Israelites (Num. 13:3,8), but Moses renamed him Joshua (Num. 3:16). Moses sent him and eleven others out to spy out the land. All twelve spies experienced the same land. The initial report said, "We went into the land to which you sent us, and it does flow with milk and honey" (Num. 13:26). They displayed Exhibit 1: A single bunch of grapes so large it had to be carried on a pole by two men. The Israelities were impressed. The report went on to page two which began with a "but."

"But the people who live there are powerful, and the cities are fortified and very large" (Num. 13:28). "We seemed like grasshoppers in our own eyes, and we looked the same to them" (Num. 13:33). This must have been an emotional roller coaster to the people of Israel.

CHOICE 2: Pick the Future Rather Than the Past

The minority report offered by Joshua and Caleb was upbeat. "We should go up and take possession of the land for we can certainly do it" (Num. 13:30). By this time, however, the hearts of the people had melted with fear.

Today, there are majority reporters ("Isn't mid-life awful!") and the minority reporters ("Isn't mid-life wonderful!"). Who are you going to believe: the *whiners* who hate being forty-something or the *winners* who are making the most of it?

A lot of people want to go back to the past. That was why God put cherubim to guard the entrance to the Garden of Eden. Thomas Merton reminded readers, "In order to be true to God and to ourselves we must break with the familiar, established and secure norms and go off into the unknown."[3] Daniel Levinson, theorist on mid-life, concluded that this period has the following fundamental tasks: (1) "to *question* and *reappraise* the existing structure; (2) to *search* for new possibilities in self and world; and (3) to *modify* the present structure enough so that a new one can be formed."[4] Some of us prevent good from coming into our lives by clinging tightly to the past.

Think of it this way, if you wanted to drive to the city nearest your home — how far would you get if you used only your rearview mirror? The rearview mirror is only for occasional use. Fortysomethings need to keep this in mind.

Maybe the first 3.9 decades have not been so good. You may agree with Bender, "My life was like a crazy quilt, a pattern I hated, with scattered, unrelated, stimulating fragments going off in its own direction."[5]

But will you let the past be a tutor, a resource pile? According to Alan Jones, in our movement toward the future God has prepared, "everything that has happened to us is a potential gift: our wounds, our disappointments, our idiosyncrasies, and our failures."[6]

That's why I like stained glass windows. The most beautiful windows are made from broken pieces of glass shaped by a master craftsman. God specializes in creating masterpieces out of broken pieces.

CHOICE 3: Focus on the Opportunity

While "problems" exist in mid-life, as chapter two pointed out, don't miss the glorious opportunities waiting to be seized and enjoyed. One fortysomething wrote:

Our forties bring a certain amount of comfort and purpose. You know better than ever what you can and cannot kid yourself about. You understand that while you may not have all the time in the world to do what you want to do, you've still got a lot. And most of all, hour by hour, day by day, you find yourself running into situations that you have experienced before, so you know how better to handle them.

This is the type of optimism that led Lee Eisenberg to exclaim, "Let's hear it for middle age!"[7]

Why can we be so optimistic? Because God is with us. That's what the Bible tells us, page after page. Wherever you find yourself—prison, wilderness, slavery, the king's palace—God is there with you. As Bill Ratcliff said, when "we feel the presence of God," in such places, "then we are able to relax and focus on what we need to learn and do in the wilderness."[8]

Consider the following letter Ann Landers received:

Last July my husband decided he was in love with his best friend's ex-wife and asked for a divorce. [Strike #1] The divorce was final on October 12. They married on October 20. [Strike #2] The following morning I had a heart attack. [Strike #3] I found out it happens to forty-year-old women, as well as sixty-five-year-old men.

Normally, in life as in baseball, "Three strikes and you are out!" But not for this courageous woman.

Since then my life has taken a 360 degree turn. I no longer smoke. I joined Weight Watchers and lost fifty-eight pounds. I watch my salt, cholesterol, fat intake and exercise daily. How do I feel? Wonderful! For the first time in my life, I know what good health is.

What I thought was the worst tragedy of my life turned out to be a blessing.[9]

This fortysomething ignored the opportunity to moan, "Isn't it awful!" Instead, she seized the opportunity to take charge of her life.

CHOICE 4: Keep Your Arms and Hearts Open
Life has a wonderful way of delivering surprises and blessings. I can stand with my arms folded across my chest and dare

someone to approach me. Or I can choose to stand with my arms open wide. By doing the latter, it means someone *could* hit me in the stomach. But I prefer to expect that someone will walk into my arms and hug me.

Many fortysomethings are going through this season with their hands clenched in anger. We can't receive gifts when our hands are clenched.

One of my favorite stories comes from Urban Holmes, former dean of the University of the South. In his book, *Spirituality for Ministry*, Holmes relates the story of a brilliant professor whose son was killed in an accident. The distraught professor—tested as he had never been before—disappeared from campus. He returned one evening at a seminary banquet. He asked the dean if he could say a few words.

"Ladies and gentlemen," he began, "in the past few weeks I have been to the bottom." He paused to regain his emotions. "But tonight I am happy to report that the bottom is solid!"[10]

This is the testimony of thousands of fortysomethings after divorce, death of a spouse, death of a child, bankruptcy, or rape. In the I can't-believe-this-is-happening moments of life, we too discover that the bottom is solid.

CHOICE 5: Choose Your Own Direction

In 1972 Mark Spitz sizzled up and down the Olympic pool in Munich. When the games were over, he could hardly stand because of the seven gold medals around his neck.

He had a future: there was talk of a movie, he had a ninety-nine year contract with Schick, Inc. Gone were his plans for dental school. He was a celebrity! But in the nearly two decades since Munich, life hasn't turned out the way he thought it would.

Recently reports began to circulate that Mark Spitz was back in the pool. Probably trying to fight the mid-life weight gains. "No," said Mark, between laps, "I'm doing a comeback."

"Get real!" the sports commentators quipped when Mark Spitz declared he wants to swim on the U.S. team in Barcelona in 1992. Impossible! One writer said, "Has he just been marinating in chlorine too long?"[11]

Spitz told Sam Allas of *Time*, "I hear people say, 'I should have done this and that.' They rattle off twenty different reasons why they didn't do something. Almost 100 percent of the time they were capable of doing exactly what they said they should have done. But they didn't."[12]

Mark Spitz will not have to make the team to have been successful. He may, in the process, help some of us redefine what forty-year-olds can do. Hodding Carter, in examining Spitz's goal, cited a powerful passage from *Heroes of the Olympics:* "It isn't mere skill or physical strength that wins Olympic victories. But *it is the desire to use that talent,* sometimes in the face of great odds, that makes heroes of the Olympics (emphasis mine).[13]

Whether Spitz makes the U.S. team or not, he will have tried. What's your arena? What talents do you have a desire to use? Will you try?

CHOICE 6: Challenge the Aging Myth

Remember how old "forty" seemed to you when you were a teen? A college student? Such is the power of myth. Someone has said that the two saddest words in the English language are, "If only." Erica Jong wrote, "When I was twenty, forty-five seemed an intolerably venerable age, an age to retire to one's countryseat and have a last long love affair with one's garden."[14]

"Now," Miss Jong continues, "that I have reached that venerable age, it seems — if not the quintessence of youth — then at least nowhere close to middle age, whatever that might be. I've never felt better, eaten more sensibly . . . or exercised more . . . at forty-five I know what I want and who I am . . . I feel younger than I ever did at twenty."[15]

Much of the aging myth has been debunked by Ronald Reagan, who was the country's oldest President, leaving office at eighty. Yet, he chopped wood, rode a horse, and still wore the same tuxedo he wore forty years ago. No wonder Americans, particularly in their sixties and seventies, are redefining the boundaries of aging. Although some claim "successful aging" is an oxymoron others are proving it daily.[16]

Joshua went against the odds and against his peers who were unwilling to go up; who rebelled against the command of the Lord; and grumbled in their tents (Deut. 1:26). Some Jews were willing to be victims of the newly spun myth about their opponent's size, but not Joshua. He brought back a report "according to my convictions" (Josh. 14:7). You may have to do the same; those who follow the Lord *wholeheartedly* as Joshua did often have to be courageous with their peers.

Moses appealed to the Israelites with three directives: (1) Go up and take possession of the land; (2) Do not be afraid; and (3) Do not be discouraged because, "the Lord is going before you" (Deut. 1:30).

Joshua, a fortysomething, chose his own direction. As a result, Moses swore to him, "The land on which your feet have walked will be your inheritance and that of your children forever" (Josh. 14:9).

Moses' directives apply to us: do not be afraid and do not be discouraged! Today is a good day to look yourself in the mirror and ask, "How can I challenge the myth?"

As Christian fortysomethings, we can particularly challenge the myth because we know that God is with us. A single adult, Isaac Watt, could write, "O God our help in ages past, Our hope for years to come, Our shelter from the stormy blast, And our eternal home!"

The second verse explains why we can trust, "Under the shadow of Thy throne, Still may we dwell secure; Sufficient is Thine arm alone, And our defense is sure."

We as fortysomethings should not be resting in our own strength, but in His.

CHOICE 7: Aim for Something That Will Make a Difference!

In preparation for this writing, I read a novel, *50* by Avery Corman, the story of Dave Gardiner, a sportswriter who became a big corporate consultant. Eventually, he gave up the security and benefits to return to the daily hassle of writing a sports column. When asked why, he responded, "I love the Mike O'Briens and the Tony Rossellis [players] and the ball games. And I wasn't as good a writer as I could be. I hadn't done my best yet. I can be better."[17]

Those words haunt me. Have I at forty-three "done my best yet?" Can I be a more effective speaker, a better friend?

The hunger for money has captured the creativity of today's best and brightest the way the dream of ending the Vietnam war challenged my generation. Some of the brightest minds have been harnassed for underwriting corporate greed in exchange for big salaries, a place in the fast lane, and ultimately an ulcer and a gold watch.

One rabbi asked a member of his congregation, "Why are you always in such a hurry?"

"Easy," the member answered, "I'm running after success."

"That's a good answer," that Rabbi nodded, "*if* you assume that those blessings are somewhere ahead of you." The member stared at his rabbi. "But isn't it possible that these blessings are behind you, that they are looking for you, and the more you run, the harder you make it for them to find you?"[18]

Increasingly, people in mid-life are becoming refugees from the fast track. They have empty souls but fat bank accounts and are looking for meaning, significance, and tenderness.

The mid-life crisis for many of us is a cry from some quiet canyon of our soul, a longing to know that we have made and can make a difference. We are desperate for an affirmation that our lives have been and are worth living.

My Jewish neighbors tell a wonderful story about the Great Judgment. God, they say, will not say to you, "Why weren't you Moses? Why weren't you Joshua? Why weren't you Jeremiah?" Rather, God will say, "Why weren't you *you?*"

Growing numbers of faith leaders are convinced that Americans are not so afraid of dying as they are of living. Gail Howard asks, "If you knew Jesus was coming tomorrow, would it make you any less afraid to do the things you were afraid to do today? Perhaps we need the kind of belief that gives us the courage to be the person we would be knowing that today is the last time we would be given the opportunity" [to make a difference].[19]

Don't waste this season.

Profile of a Fortysomething: Ben Milam (1788–1835). This single adult was forty-seven when he stepped into history. He chose his own direction and aimed for something that would make a difference.

A band of courageous Texans were camped near San Antonio on December 4, 1835. Ben Milan had been sent by another single adult, Stephen F. Austin, founder of the Texas colony, to scout out the Mexican troops and to determine the possibility of the Texans taking San Antonio.

Ben Milam had a right as a fortysomething to be bitter with life. A prominent merchant in Texas, on one trip to Europe, he searched London's best stores and shops for gifts to bring home to his Texas financeé. When he returned home, her sister broke the news that she had married another man.

Ben was devastated. But he summoned his wits and said, "I am going to give you these things I bought for her; I haven't time for women anyway. My country surely must need me." The rest of his life, Ben focused on one passion: freedom for Texas.

That cold December night, when he arrived in the camp, he found men ready to desert, to head home without fighting for San Antonio. Some argued that such an attack would be suicidal; others insisted that they wait until more reinforcements arrived.

Ben Milam recognized his moment. With the toe of his boot he drew a line on the ground. Facing the men he demanded: "Who will go with old Ben Milam to San Antonio?"

Three hundred and one men jumped to their feet. The next morning, the Mexicans were stunned by the ferocious attack of the Texans.

Three days later, on December 7, Ben Milam died for the cause. But eventually the Mexicans surrendered, and the ambitious Texans took a big step toward independence. Ben Milam, a fortysomething, made a difference.[20]

CHOICE 8: Trust the God Who Never Ages

Dr. Ralph Earle, a brilliant New Testament scholar who was one of the major influences in the development of the *New International Version* of the Bible, frequently relates the story of John G. Paton, a pioneer missionary to the New Hebrides. Paton quickly discovered that the Islanders had words for house, tree, stone, and the like but no words for love, joy, and peace. Worse, they had no word for *believe.* How could he possibly translate the Bible into their language?

One day, John Paton sat in his small hut, frustrated by the progress of his linguistic studies, when an old man entered and slumped down in a chair, seemingly exhausted from a long journey. The old man remarked, "I'm leaning my whole weight on this chair."

"What did you say?" John asked.

"I'm leaning my whole weight on this chair."

Paton cried out joyfully: "That's it!" That's it!" He had found a way to translate the biblical promise of belief in God. "From that day forward," Dr. Earle observed, "believe in Jesus" became "lean your whole weight on Jesus."[21]

How can you survive this fortysomething experience? By leaning all your weight on the Jesus who will accompany us through the ups and the downs of mid-life. My pastor wrote me when I turned forty: " . . . do not fear the age forty. I must tell you the best part of my life has been since forty. And in many ways God has only been preparing you up until now for the rich ministry that the fourth and fifth decade of your life will have.[22]

CHOICE 9: Focus on the Father Not the Crisis

There were several crises in Jesus' ministry. His disciples had a hard time totally committing themselves to Him. Although

Peter said, "We have left everything to follow You!" (Mark 10:28), his declaration followed an argument on the road to Capernaum, "about who was the greatest" (Mark 9:33). Maybe the disciples were early yuppies. Jesus explained that first they must be servants. Then and now, such ideas fall on deaf ears.

Later in Mark's Gospel, James and John, came to Jesus, saying, "Teacher, we want You to do for us whatever we ask" (Mark 10:35). Which is the way a lot of fortysomethings come to Jesus today.

"What do you want Me to do for you?" He asked (Mark 10:36).

"Let one of us sit at Your right and the other at Your left in Your glory" (Mark 10:37). The discussion caused the other ten to be indignant with the brothers. Obviously the concept of servanthood was alien to James and John. We can be so busy thinking about other things during the mid-life that we overlook Jesus' invitation to be servants.

Jesus survived so many crises, my pastor friend Ken Smith says, because He focused on the Father, *not* on the crisis. Jesus, aware that His death was fast approaching, prayed, not "Father, save Me from this hour" but "Father, glorify Your name!" (John 12:28)

Dare we pray the same thing? The popular chorus says, "In my life, Lord, be glorified; be glorified." Dare we substitute *mid-life* for life, and invite God to be glorified?

CHOICE 10: Do Something!
One last exercise may most effectively wrap up our examination of mid-life crisis and transition.

On a blank sheet of paper, draw a horizontal line from right to left. This is your lifeline. At the far left, write the year of your birth. At the far right write the year you plan to die. Now, somewhere along this line write in the year you are reading *Fortysomething and Single*.

Here's the way I completed this task:

1947 _____ 1991 _____ 2047

Now, below the line, draw a "basket" connecting the present year and the year you plan to die. Sidney Simon in *Getting Unstuck* suggests, that this basket represents the life you have to live. "It can be filled with all the opportunities, challenges, joys and experiences still ahead of you."[23] Now, answer the following questions and place the answers "inside" the basket:

1. What do I want to do with the life I have left?
2. What do I want to experience?
3. What do I want to witness?
4. What do I want to learn?
5. What do I want to be part of?
6. What do I want to change, shape, leave better than I found it?
7. What do I want to do with the rest of my life?[24]

In my workshops with single adults I have frequently used this exercise and have listened to the groans when I said, "the year you plan to die." However, I have also watched amazement sweep across the faces of fortysomethings as they completed the task.

Hopefully, you will have to enlarge the "net" time and again to accommodate your priorities.

Remember: It is never too late to be a fortysomething!

CONCLUSION

Where will you be when you get to where you are going? Will it be the place you have longed for and dreamed about?

Who will you be when you get to where you are going? Will you be comfortable with that person—even if it is still "just" you? Will that you be wiser and warmer, more tender, caring, and committed to the things that Jesus was committed to? That depends on your decision. . . . the choices you make. Your major goal is to befriend this decade of your life.

You must do the following. Admit that you are forty. Pick the future rather than the past. Focus on the opportunities of this decade. Keep your arms and heart open to life's surprises.

Trust people. Aim for something that will make a difference. Trust the God who has been with you. And finally, sing those glorious words of Isaac Watts, "O God, our help in ages past, our hope in years to come."

My pastor, Jeff Black, says that there is an element in us that God respects and is willing to suffer with so that we can love Him and become all that He longs for us to be.

After writing the first draft of this book, I read William Johnson's *The Wounded Stag.* I found these words so challenging:

The great challenge is to remain open to love, to remain open to change, and to remain open to growth.

Sometimes (perhaps three or four times in a life-time) metanoia may take the form of a great upheaval, an inner revolution, a violent shock through which one painfully yet joyfully acquires a new vision and sets out on a new path. These are times of crisis when one realizes that this life of love is an awful risk, leading us to a place we do not know by a path we know not."[25]

A PRAYER FOR FORTYSOMETHINGS

May the Lord bless you and keep you.
May the Lord make His face to shine upon you
and be gracious unto you.
May God give you grace never to sell yourself short;
grace to risk something big for something good;
grace to remember that the world is now too dangerous
for anything but truth and too small for anything but
love.
So,
May God take your minds and think through them,
May God take your lips and speak through them.
May God take your hearts and set them on fire.
Amen.

—Stephen Shoemaker

QUESTIONS

1. Who will you be when you get where you're going?
2. How will you see yourself at the end of this season?
3. How have you experienced God's grace in this season?
4. What can you do to make a difference for the good?
5. What notions/fantasies/tales have you discarded as a result of reading this book?
6. What is the "land" to be conquered in your life?
7. Have you done your best yet?

To contact Harold Ivan Smith regarding speaking engagements, please write or call Michael McKinney
    McKinney Associates
    P.O. Box 5162
    Louisville, Kentucky 40205
    (502) 583-8222

Appendix A
FRIEND OF A FORTYSOMETHING SURVEY

Today is August 4

Dear _____ :

On August 21 I will be experiencing my fortieth birthday. It is something of a milestone and seems to be the time to give some serious thought to the next ten years of my life and career. But it also seems a good time to tinker and fine-tune. To take a good hard look at what it means to be me.

We've been friends for some time now. That's why I feel free to ask a favor of you. Could you take some time, in the next couple weeks, to give me some advice. From your vantage point what are my strengths? What are my weaknesses? How could our friendship be improved? Where do you think I should invest my energies? If you could help me see one thing about myself that has frustrated or concerned you, what would that be?

I wish turning forty was like turning twenty or thirty. There is a different sense of seriousness about it.

It may make your task a little easier to know the Lord and I have already had some discussions on this topic. I realize you may be a bit hesitant to do what I am asking, but I want you to be honest.

It may be that you will need more than the page that is enclosed. Feel free to write more.

So, that's my request. I hope you will feel comfortable in responding. I will look forward to reading your responses but also in talking with you if there are some things you would rather not put on paper.

I hope today will be a good day for you.

Harold Ivan Smith

Strengths	*Weaknesses*
1. _____	1. _____
2. _____	2. _____
3. _____	3. _____
4. _____	4. _____
5. _____	5. _____

How could our friendship be strengthened? _____

_____

_____

_____

_____

Where should I invest my energies in the next ten years?

_____

_____

_____

Your advice to me about turning forty _____

_____

_____

_____

FORTYSOMETHING BOOK LIST

These pilgrims wrote books that will make a difference in your spiritual journey through a season called Fortysomething:

1. Augustine. *Confessions*
2. Baille, John. *A Diary of Private Prayer*
3. Bender, Sue. *Plain and Simple: A Woman's Journey to the Amish*
4. Bonhoeffer, Dietrich. *Letters and Papers from Prison*
   _____. *The Cost of Discipleship*
   _____. *Life Together*
5. *The Book of Common Prayer*
6. Brainerd, David. *David Brainerd's Journal*
7. Buechner, Frederick. *Then and Now*
   _____. *This Sacred Journey*
   _____. *Telling the Truth*
8. Colson, Chuck. *Born Again*
   _____. *Loving God*

9. Edwards, Gene. *The Inward Journey*
   ———. *A Tale of Three Kings*
10. Edwards, Tilden. *Spiritual Friend*
11. Eliott, Elisabeth. *Shadow of the Almighty*
    ———. *Loneliness*
12. Foster, Richard. *Celebration of Discipline*
    ———. *Freedom of Simplicity*
13. Griffin, Emile. *Clinging: The Experience of Prayer*
14. Guyon, Madame. *Spiritual Letters*
15. Hammarsjkold, Dag. *Markings*
16. Harper, Steven. *Embracing the Spirit*
17. Howatch, Susan. *Glittering Images*
18. Job, Reuben P. and Norman Shawchuck. *A Guide to Prayer for Ministers and Other Servants*
19. Jones, Alan. *Exploring Spiritual Direction*
    ———. *Soul Making*
20. Kelly, Thomas. *A Testament of Devotion*
21. Kelsey, Morton. *Adventure Inward*
    ———. *The Other Side of Silence*
22. Kempis, Thomas à *The Imitation of Christ*
23. Kushner, Harold. *When All You've Ever Wanted Isn't Enough*
24. Law, William. *A Serious Call to a Devout and Holy Life*
25. Lawrence, Brother. *Practicing the Presence of God*
26. Lewis, C.S. *Mere Christianity*
    ———. *Surprised by Joy*
    ———. *A Grief Observed*
27. Manning, Brennan. *The Lion and the Lamb*
    ———. *The Ragamuffin Gospel*
28. Merton, Thomas. *Contemplative Prayer*
    ———. *Twelve Story Mountain*
29. Muggeridge, Malcolm. *Confessions of a Twentieth Century Pilgrim*
30. Mutto, Susan Annette. *Pathways of Spiritual Living*
    ———. *Blessings That Make Us Be*
    ———. *Celebrating the Single Life*
31. Nouwen, Henri. *In the Name of Jesus*
    ———. *All Things Made New*
    ———. *The Wounded Healer*

32. Peck, M. Scott. *The Road Less Traveled*
33. Pennington, Basil. *Called*
34. Seamands, David. *Healing for Damaged Emotions*
35. Sinetar, Marsha. *Ordinary People as Monks and Mystics*
36. Swanson, Kenneth. *Uncommon Prayer: Approaching Intimacy with God*
37. Underhill, Evelyn. *The Spiritual Life*
38. Vanauken, Sheldon. *A Severe Mercy*
39. Wiederkehr, Macrina. *A Tree Full of Angels*
40. Willard, Dallas. *Spirit of the Disciplines*

A p p e n d i x C

FORTY LITERARY FRIENDS FOR FORTYSOMETHINGS

This list was developed through examining recommended reading lists from Clifton Fadiman's *The Lifetime Reading Plan;* the American Library Association's *Outstanding Books for the College Bound* [Chicago, ALA, 1984]; J. Sherwood Weber, *Good Reading: A Guide for Serious Readers* [21st ed; 1980]; "Students Get the Word on What to Read," *U.S. News and World Report*, 20 August 1984 and 28 September 1987; consultation with Dr. Elva McAllaster, Poet-in-Residence, Greenville College and Roy Carlisle, President of Mills House.

1. Austen, Jane. *Pride and Prejudice*
2. Bronte, Emily. *Wuthering Heights*
3. Browning, Elizabeth Barrett. *Sonnets from the Portugese*
4. Camus, Albert. *The Plague*
   ———. *The Stranger*
5. Carroll, Lewis. *Alice's Adventure in the Wonderland*
   ———. *Through the Looking Glass*

6. Cather, Willa. *My Antonia*
   ———. *Death Comes for the Archbishop*
7. Cervantes. *Don Quixote*
8. Conrad, Joseph. *Lord Jim*
   ———. *Nostromo*
9. Cooper, James Fenimore. *The Last of the Mohicans*
10. Dante. *The Inferno*
    ———. *The Divine Comedy*
11. Defoe, Daniel. *Robinson Crusoe*
12. Dickens, Charles. *David Copperfield*
    ———. *A Tale of Two Cities*
    ———. *Great Expectations*
13. Donne, John. *Selected Works*
14. Dostoyevski, Fedor. *The Brothers Karamazov*
    ———. *Crime and Punishment*
    ———. *The Idiot*
15. Eliot, George. *Middlemarch*
    ———. *The Mill on the Floss*
16. Faulkner, William. *As I Lay Dying*
    ———. *The Sound and the Fury*
17. Forster, E.M. *A Passage to India*
18. Frost, Robert. *Collected Poems*
19. Greene, Graham. *The Power and the Glory*
20. Hardy, Thomas. *The Return of the Native*
    ———. *Tess of the D'Ubbervilles*
21. Hawthorne, Nathaniel. *The Scarlet Letter*
    ———. *The House of Seven Gables*
22. Hemingway, Ernest. *The Old Man and the Sea*
    ———. *For Whom the Bell Tolls*
23. Hugo, Victor. *Les Misérables*
24. Kafka, Franz. *The Trial*
25. Mann, Thomas. *The Magic Mountain*
26. Melville, Herman. *Moby Dick*
    ———. *Billy Budd*
27. Milton, John. *Paradise Lost*
28. Orwell, George. *Animal Farm*
    ———. *Nineteen-Eighty-Four*
29. Rabelais, Francois. *Gargantua and Pabtagruel*

30. Scott, Sir Walter. *Ivanhoe*
31. Shakespeare. *Hamlet*
    _____. *Henry V*
    _____. *Julius Caesar*
    _____. *King Lear*
    _____. *Macbeth*
    _____. *A Midsummer Night's Dream*
32. Solzhenitsyn, Aleksandr. *The Gulag Archipelago*
    _____. *A Day in the Life of Ivan Denisovich*
33. Steinbeck, John. *Of Mice and Men*
    _____. *The Grapes of Wrath*
34. Stevenson, Robert Louis. *The Strange Case of Dr. Jeykll and Mr. Hyde*
35. Stowe, Harriet Beecher. *Uncle Tom's Cabin*
36. Swift, Jonathan. *Gulliver's Travels*
37. Thackery, William Makepeace. *Vanity Fair*
38. Thorèau, Henry David. *Walden*
39. Tolstoy, Leo. *War and Peace*
40. Twain, Mark. *Huckleberry Finn*
    _____. *Tom Sawyer*

Notes

Chapter 1

1. J. Bill Ratliff, *When You Are Facing Change* (Louisville: Westminster/John Knox Press, 1990), 93.
2. Sue Bender, *Plain and Simple: A Woman's Journey to the Amish* (San Francisco: Harper and Row, 1989), xii.
3. Rainer Maria Rilke, *Letters to a Young Poet*, trans. M.D. Herter Norton, rev. ed. (New York: W.W. Norton, 1962), 35.
4. Ruth A. Tucker and Walter Liefeld, *Daughters of the Church* (Grand Rapids: Zondervan Publishing House, 1987), 304–306.
5. Dag Hammarskjold, *Markings*, trans. Leif Sjoberg and W.H. Auden (New York: Alfred A. Knopf, Inc., 1965), 89.
6. Horace Porter, "Address at the Commemorative Exercises in Honor of John Paul Jones, 24 April 1906, U.S. Naval Academy, Annapolis, Maryland. (Washington, D.C.: Government Printing Office, 1907), 30.

Chapter 2

1. Jane Fonda and Megan McCarthy, *Women Coming of Age* (New York: Simon and Schuster, Inc., 1984), 21.
2. Jerry Gerber, Janet Wolff, Walter Klores, and Gene Brown. *Lifetrends: The Future of Baby Boomers and Other Old Americans* (New York: Macmillan Publishing Co., Inc., 1989), 6.
3. Ibid.
4. Daniel J. Levinson et al., *The Seasons of a Man's Life* (New York: Ballantine, 1978), 57.
5. Gerber, *Lifetrends*, 21.
6. Robert J. Havinghurst, *Developmental Tasks and Education*. 3rd ed. (New York: Longman, 1972), 83–94.
7. Ibid., 95–106.
8. Levinson, *Seasons*, 195–197.

9. Anne Rosenfeld and Elizabeth Stark, "The Prime of Our Lives," *Psychology Today*, 21 May 1987, 68, 66.

10. Ibid., 68.

11. Ibid.

12. Ibid., 66.

13. Gerber, *Lifetrends*, 198–201.

14. Nancy Meyer, *The Male Mid-Life Crisis: Fresh Starts After Forty* (New York: Doubleday & Co., Inc., 1978), 35.

15. Russell Segal, "Questions and Answers: The Facts of Mid-Life," *Men's Health*, April 1990, 42.

16. Levinson, *Seasons*, 18.

17. Rachel Z. Dulin, *A Crown of Glory: A Biblical View of Aging,* (New York: Paulist Press, 1988), 18.

18. Ibid., 22–35.

19. Janis Bellack and Penny A. Mabford, *Nursing Assessment: A Multidimensional Approach* (Monterey: Wadsworth Health Services, 1984), 131; Nancy Belloc and Linda Breslow, "Relationship of Physical Health Status and Health Practices," *Preventative Medicine*, 1 (1972): 409–521.

20. Fonda, and McCarthy, *Coming of Age*, 27.

21. Domeena C. Renshaw, "Sex and Eating Disorders," *Medical Aspects of Human Sexuality* 24 (April 1990): 68.

22. George Kaluger and Meriem Fair Kaluger, *Human Development: The Span of Life*, 2nd ed. (St. Louis: C.V. Mosby, 1979), 417.

23. Ibid., 420.

24. Anne Morrow Lindbergh, *Gifts from the Sea* (New York: Vantage Pr., Inc., 1975), 87–88.

25. Kaluger, *Human Development*, 398.

26. Joseph V. Bailey. *The Serenity Principle: Finding Inner Peace in Recovery* (San Francisco: Harper and Row Pubs., Inc., 1990), 15.

27. Ibid., 86; Robert Kastenbaum, *Humans Developing: A Lifespan Perspective* (Boston: Allyn and Bacon, 1979), 564.

28. Meyer, *Mid-Life Crisis*, 110.

29. Ibid., 112.

30. Jack Gordon, "Who Killed Corporate Loyalty?", *Training*, March 1990, 27.

31. Kaluger, *Human Development*, 409–10.

32. Levinson, *Seasons*, 72.

33. Ibid., 60–61.

34. Elliott Jaques, *Work, Creativity, and Social Justice* (London: International Universities Press, 1970), n.p., quoted in Levinson, *Seasons*, 196.

35. Levinson, *Seasons*, 42.

36. Ibid., 37.

37. Ibid., 49.

Chapter 3

1. Rosenfeld and Stark, "Prime Of Our lives," 71.

2. Wendy Green, *Getting Things Done: Eva Burrows, A Biography* (Hants, England: Marshall Pickering, 1988), 42–43.

3. L. David Duff, *The Ramsey Covenant: A Story About Evelyn Ramsey* (Kan-

162   Fortysomething and Single

sas City: Nazarene Publishing House, 1985), 26–27.
4. Ibid.
5. Barbara Hudson Powers, *The Henrietta Mears Story* (Old Tappan, N.J. Fleming H. Revell Co., 1965), 116–17.
6. Ibid., 117.
7. Catherine Clinton, *The Plantation Mistress: Woman's World in the Old South* (New York: Pantheon Bks., 1982), 39.
8. Mae Elizabeth Harveson, *Catherine Esther Beecher: Pioneer Educator* (Philadelphia: University of Pennsylvania Press, 1932), 98.
9. N. Louis Bailey, "Joseph Alston," *Biographical Dictionary of the South Carolina House of Representatives* (Columbia: University of South Carolina Press, 1984), 32–35.
10. John P. Splinter, *Second Chapter: New Beginnings After Divorce or Separation* (Grand Rapids: Baker Book House, 1987), 146; Robert C. Williamson, *Marriage and Family Relations* (New York: John Wiley and Sons, Inc. 1966), 554, 254.
11. Lowell H. Harrison, *George Rogers Clark and the War in the West* (Lexington: University of Kentucky Press, 1976), 108–09.
12. John F. Walvoord and Roy B. Zuck, eds., *The Bible Knowledge Commentary* (Wheaton, Ill.: Victor Books, 1986), 247–49.

Chapter 4
1. Ida R. Bellgrade, Mary Bethune, and James Weldon Johnson, *Black Heroes and Heroines* (Pine Bluff, Ark.: Bell Enterprises, 1979), 98.
2. Ratliff, *Facing Change*, 12.
3. John Nesbitt and Patricia Auburdene, *Megatrends 2000: Ten New Directions for the 1990s* (New York: William Morrow & Co., Inc., 1990), 272.
4. Ibid., 270–71.
5. Billy Graham, untitled essay in Phillip L. Berman, ed., *The Courage of Conviction* (New York: Ballantine, 1985), 107.
6. Andrew Greeley, "Introduction" in Ibid., xv.
7. George Gallup, Jr. and George O'Connell, *Who Do Americans Say That I Am?* (Philadelphia: Westminster Press, 1986), 64.
8. Charles W. Colson, "A Call to Rescue Yuppies," *Christianity Today*, 17 May 1985, 20.
9. "Churches Take Close Look at How They Teach Religion," *Kansas City Star*, 27 May 1990, Sec. E.
10. Philip S. Watson, *Let God Be God: An Interpretation of the Theology of Martin Luther* (Philadelphia: Muhlenberg, 1949), 85.
11. Ibid., 170.
12. Dietrich Bonhoeffer, *The Cost of Discipleship*, rev. ed. (New York: Macmillan Publishing Co., Inc., 1963), 47.
13. Ibid., pp. 47–48.
14. *The Book of Common Prayer* (New York: Seabury Pr., Inc., 1979), 416–17.
15. Ibid., p. 66.
16. William M. Greathouse, "Apostle's Creed," in *The Beacon Dictionary of Theology*, ed. Richard S. Taylor (Kansas City: Beacon Hill Press, 1983), 46.
17. J.B. Phillips, *Your God Is Too Small* (New York: Macmillan Publishing Co., Inc., 1987).

18. Bruce Larson, *No Longer Strangers* (Waco: Word, Inc., 1971), 56.
19. Norman Mable, *Popular Hymns and Their Writers* (London: Independent Press, 1951), 58–61. See also John Bruce, *The Poetical Works of William Cowper*, vol. 1 (London: Bell and Daldy York Street, 1886).
20. Robert E.B. Baylor Papers, 13 April 1871, Baylor University Archives.
21. Ibid. See also "Robert Emmet Bledsoe Baylor," *Dictionary of American Biography*, ed. Allen Johnson, vol. 1, part 2 (New York: Charles Scribner's Sons, 1964), 77–78.
22. Arnold E. Airhart, "Holy Spirit," in the *Beacon Dictionary*, Taylor, 262–264.
23. L.C. Randolph, *Francis Asbury* (Nashville: Abingdon Press, 1966), 220.

Chapter 5
1. Nesbitt and Auburdene, *Megatrends 2000*, 277.
2. James Davison Hunter, *American Evangelicalism: Contemporary Religion and the Quandary of Modernity* (Brunswick, N.J.: Rutgers University Press, 1983), 11, 18.
3. Bill Hybels, *Honest to God: Becoming an Authentic Christian* (Grand Rapids: Zondervan Publishing House, 1990), 181.
4. "Missionary Featured at the Church of the Nazarene," biographical sketch prepared by the Department of World Missions, Church of the Nazarene, Kansas City, Missouri; "Cory Abke: "Interview: President Don Owens," *Accent on MidAmerica Nazarene College*, Summer 1988, backpage.
5. Stephen B. Oates, *Let the Trumpet Sound: The Life of Martin Luther King, Jr.* (New York: Harper and Row Pubs., Inc., 1982), 223.
6. Tom Sine, *Taking Discipleship Seriously: A Radical Biblical Approach* (Valley Forge, Pa.: Judson Press, 1985), 23.
7. Vance Havner, *Though I Walk Through the Valley* (Old Tappan, N.J.: Fleming H. Revell Co., 1978), 124–25.
8. J. Gilchrist Lawson, *Deeper Experiences of Famous Christians* (Anderson, Ind.: Warner Press, 1911), 317.
9. Ibid.
10. *Single Adult Ministry Information (SEMI) Newsletter* published by Institute of Singles Dynamics, 6 April 1990, 4.
11. Ratliff, *Facing Change*, 14.

Chapter 6
1. "Dean Bertha Munro—Her Life," *Christian Scholar* Memorial Edition, (February 1983): 1.
2. Ibid.
3. Bernie Siegel, "The Relation of the Mind and Body in the Healing Process, Temple B'nai Jehudah, Kansas City, Missouri, lecture, 12 Sept. 1989.
4. Norman Vincent Peale and William Thomas Buckley, *The American Character* (Old Tappan, N.J.: Fleming H. Revell Co., 1988), 187–88.
5. Ibid.
6. Robert Bly, *The Little Book of the Human Shadow* (San Francisco: Harper and Row Pubs., Inc., 1988), 18.
7. Sidney Jourard, *The Transparent Self*, rev. ed. (New York: Van Nostrand,

1971), 59.

8. Ibid., 5.

9. Stephen Shoemaker, sermon, Crescent Hill Baptist Church, Louisville, Ky., 27 May 1990.

10. Gordon MacDonald, *Restoring Your Spiritual Passion* (Nashville: Oliver-Nelson, 1986), 127.

11. Ibid., 136.

12. "Barbara Jordan," *Current Biography: 1974,* ed. Charles Moritz (New York: H.W. Wilson, 1974), 189–92. See also Barbara Jordan, *Barbara Jordan: A Self Portrait* (New York: Doubleday & Co., Inc., 1979).

Chapter 7

1. Evelyn Underhill in *A Guide for Prayer and Ministers and Other Servants,* by Reuben P. Job and Norman Shawchuck (Nashville: The Upper Room, 1983), 320.

2. Ibid., 324.

3. Ibid.

4. Daniel Taylor, personal correspondence with author, 30 March 1989.

5. "Even Winners Battle the Blues," *U.S. News and World Report,* 20 January 1986, 55.

6. Ibid.

7. Ibid.

8. Siona Carpenter, "Mother, Daughter Get Berea Diplomas." *Lexington (Ky.) Herald-Leader,* 28 May 1990, sec. B.

9. "27 Million Americans Cannot Read This," *Personnel Administrator,* August 1989, cover.

10. Dennis Kinlaw, "Don't Ever Read a Good Book," *Christianity Today,* 18 April 1986, 10.

11. Elton Trueblood, "The Blessings of Maturity," in *The Courage to Grow Old,* ed. Phillip L. Berman (New York: Ballantine, 1989), 295.

12. Clifton Fadiman, *The Lifetime Reading Plan,* 3rd ed. (New York: Harper and Row Pubs., Inc., 1988), 1.

13. Ibid., 3.

14. *The Vision Grows: Fifty Years, 1933-1983* (Ventura, Calif.: Gospel Light, 1983), 11.

15. Peter F. Drucker, "What Can Nonprofits Teach Us?" *Review,* May 1990, 23.

16. "Dorothea Lynde Dix," *Dictionary of American Biography,* vol. 8, ed. Allen Johnson and Dumas Malone (New York: Charles Scribner's Sons, 1959), 323–25; Dorothy Clarke Wilson, *Stranger and Traveler: The Story of Dorothea Dix, American Reformer* (Boston: Little, Brown & Co., 1975), 185, 96–98, 156, 162.

17. W. David Lewis, "Emily Perkins Bissell," *Notable American Women: A Biographical Dictionary, 1607-1950,* vol. 1 (Cambridge: Belknap, 1971), 152–53.

Chapter 8

1. Bill B, *Compulsive Overeater: The Basic Text for Overeaters* (Minneapolis: CompCare, 1981), xvii-ix.

2. C.S. Lewis, *Mere Christianity* (Westwood, N.J.: Barbour and Company, 1952), 111.
3. Overeaters Anonymous, *A Guide to the 12 Steps for You and Your Sponsor* (Los Angeles: Overeaters Anonymous World Service Office, 1977), ii.
4. Bailey, *The Serenity Principle*, 59.
5. Ibid., 105.
6. Elva McAllaster, *Free to Be Single* (Chappaqua, N.Y.: Christian Herald, 1979), 275.
7. Ibid., 278.
8. Perry W. Buffington, "Those Big 'O' Birthdays," *Sky*, September 1987, 151.
9. Sandra Burkhardt and Sandie Horwitz, "How to Beat the Birthday Blues," *BH&L*, n.d., 18.
10. Kenneth Scott Latourette, *Beyond the Ranges* (Grand Rapids: Wm. B. Eerdmans Pub. Co., 1967), 153–55.
11. McAllaster, *Free*, 123.
12. Ibid.

Chapter 9

1. Norma Smith, "The Woman Who Said No to War," *MS*, March 1986, 86–89; see also Joan Hoff Wilson, "Jeannette Rankin" in *Notable American Women: The Modern Period*, ed. by Barbara Sicherman and Carol Hurd Green (Cambridge: Belknap Press, 1980), 566–68.
2. Lawrence Shames, *The Hunger for More: Searching for Values in an Age of Greed* (New York: Times Books, 1989), 27, 21.
3. "Where Consumer Credit Is Due." *Washington Post*, 21 October 1990, sec. A.
4. Terri Cole–Whittaker, *How to Have More in a Have Not World* (New York, Rawson Assocs., 1983).
5. Joe Edward Barnhart, *The Southern Baptist Holy War* (Austin: Texas Monthly Press, 1987), n.p.
6. Hugh Evan Hopkins, *Charles Simeon of Cambridge* (Grand Rapids: Wm. B. Eerdmans Pubs. Co., 1977), 63.
7. Scully Blotnick, *Ambitious Men: Their Drives, Dreams and Delusions* (New York: Viking, 1987), 3–4.
8. C.B. Axford, "Charles Hayden," *Dictionary of American Biography*, vol. 11, part 2, supplement 2, ed. Robert Livingston Schuyler and Edward T. James (New York: Charles Scribner's Sons, 1958), 292–93.
9. Robert M. Gardiner, *The Dean Whittier Guide to Personal Investing* (New York: New American Library, 1988), 44.
10. Mrs. R.W. McDonnell, *Belle Harris Bennett: Her Life Work* (Nashville: Cokesbury, 1928), 134–58.
11. Bessie Houser Nunn, "A Life Transcendent: For Use by Young People in Presenting the Belle H. Bennett Memorial," Scarritt College Archives, n.d.
12. Smith, "Woman," 86–89.

Chapter 10

1. Bartlett's *Familiar Quotations*, ed. Emily Morison Beck (Boston: Little,

Brown and Co., 1980), 908.
2. Michael W. Rubinoff, "Are You Tough Enough?" *Arizona Republic,* 19 January 1986, sec. E.
3. Joshua Herschel, *I Asked For Wonder: A Spiritual Anthology* (New York: Crossroad, 1983), xiii.
4. Ibid.
5. Daniel Taylor, "The Fear of Insignificance," *Christianity Today,* 3 February 1989, 26.
6. John Farrow, *Damien the Leper* (New York: Sheed and Ward, 1937), 98.
7. Ibid., 157.
8. Ibid., 148.
9. Ibid., 151.
10. Hans Hoekendijk, "Father Damien," *McGraw-Hill Encyclopedia of World Biography,* vol. 3 (New York: McGraw-Hill, 1973), 257.
11. "Grover Cleveland, *Dictionary of American Biography* volume 2, part 1, ed. Allen Johnson (New York: Charles Scribner's Sons, 1964), 207.
12. Harry T. Burn, "Letter to the Editor," *The West Tennessee Historical Society's Papers,* 19 (1965), 134–35; *Public Acts of the State of Tennessee, Sixty-First General Assembly,* 1919 (Jackson: McCowat-Mercer, 1919); Jim Stokley and Jeff Johnson, ed., *An Encyclopedia of East Tennessee* (Oak Ridge: Children's Museum of Oak Ridge, 1981), n.p. Stanley J. Folmsbee, Robert E. Corlew, and Enoch L. Mitchell, ed., *Tennessee, A Short History* (Knoxville. University of Tennessee Press, 1980), 453-56.
13. Lech Walesa, untitled article in Berman, *The Courage,* 231.
14. Ibid., 227.
15. Berman, *The Courage of Conviction,* xi.
16. Steve Chappie and David Talbott, *Burning Desires: Sex in America* (New York: Doubleday & Co., Inc., 1988), 321, 319; "A Fall From Grace on the Right," *U.S. News and World Report,* 25 May 1987, 27.
17. Chappie and Talbott, *Burning Desires,* 327.
18. Ibid., 312.
19. Ibid.; Lynn Rosellini, "Koop: Rebel with a Cause," *U.S. News and World Report,* 30 May 1988, 59–60.

Chapter 11
1. Sue Bender quoted in "Changing a Life After Living With the Amish," by Lou Pappas, *Raleigh News and Observer,* 24 March 1990, sec. 2D.
2. Paul Tournier, quoted in *The Freedom We Crave,* William Lenters (Grand Rapids: Wm. B. Eerdmans Pub. Co., 1985), 122.
3. Thomas Merton, *Contemplative Prayer* (Garden City, N.Y.: Doubleday—Image Books, 1971), 24.
4. Levinson, *Seasons,* 53.
5. Bender, *Plain and Simple,* 4.
6. Alan Jones, *Exploring Spiritual Direction: An Essay on Christian Friendship* (New York: Seabury Pr., Inc., 1982), 76.
7. Lee Eisenberg, "Wisdom of the Ages," *Esquire,* May 1990, 35.
8. Ratcliff, *Facing Change,* 76.
9. Ann Landers, "Woman Finds Divorce Is Blessing in Disguise," *Kansas City Star,* 12 April 1990.

10. Urban T. Holmes, III, *Spirituality for Ministry* (San Francisco: Harper and Row Pubs. Inc., 1982), 135.
11. Hodding Carter IV, "The Further Dreams of Mark Spitz," *Esquire*, May 1990, 142.
12. Sam Allas, "Interview: Testing the Limits of Middle Age," *Time*, 21 May 1990, 13.
13. Carter, "Mark Spitz," 142.
14. Erica Jong, "Is There Sex After 40?", *Vogue*, March 1987, 304
15. Ibid.
16. Marj Jackson Levin, "Breaking the Age Boundaries," *Kansas City Star*, 25 October 1987, sec. 4J.
17. Avery Corman, *50* (New York: Simon & Schuster, Inc. 1987), 248.
18. Harold S. Kushner, *When All You've Ever Wanted Isn't Enough* (New York: Summit Bks., 1986), 146.
19. Sue and Gail Howard, *I Am Afraid* (Pasadena: World-Wide Missions, 1973), back cover.
20. Dan Kubiak, *Ten Tall Texans*, 10th ed. (Austin: Balcones Company, 1985), 122–29.
21. Robert Kopp, "What Every Parent Has in Common with 3 John," sermon, First Presbyterian Church, Maumee, Ohio, 29 April 1990.
22. Millard Reed, personal correspondence with author, 31 July 1987.
23. Sidney B. Simon, *Getting Unstuck: Breaking Through Your Barriers to Change* (New York: Warner Bks., Inc., 1988), 28–30.
24. Ibid.
25. William Johnson, *The Wounded Stag* (San Francisco: Harper and Row Pubs. Inc., 1984), 81.